Fun for a Fiver in Amsterdam

Ben West has written for many newspapers and magazines including the *Guardian*, the *Independent*, the *Daily Telegraph*, *The Times*, the *Daily Mail*, the *Evening Standard* and *Reader's Digest*. He was chief property writer of the *Daily Express* and the *Sunday Express* from 1999–2001. He has appeared on numerous radio and television programmes and his work has been translated into foreign languages as varied as Korean, Czechoslovakian and Polish. He recently completed a play that has generated considerable interest in a dire pub theatre in a grim suburb of London.

Also available in Pan Books by Ben West

Fun for a Fiver in London

Ben West

Fun for a Fiver in Amsterdam

PAN BOOKS

First published 2002 by Pan Books
an imprint of Pan Macmillan Ltd
Pan Macmillan, 20 New Wharf Road, London N1 9RR
Basingstoke and Oxford
Associated companies throughout the world
www.panmacmillan.com

ISBN 0 330 48607 1

9 8 7 6 5 4 3 2 1

A CIP catalogue record for this book is available from
the British Library.

Typeset by SetSystems Ltd, Saffron Walden, Essex
Printed and bound in Great Britain by
Mackays of Chatham plc, Chatham, Kent

Contents

Introduction

The person who said that the best things in life are free has clearly never driven a factory-fresh Ferrari. But that doesn't mean to say that obtaining something without paying much or anything for it isn't gratifying. Especially when the basic art of existing can be prohibitive at the best of times.

Whatever your age and interests, whether you are a resident wishing to discover more of your city, or a visitor who, after shelling out for transport, board and lodgings doesn't wish to also have to travel the expensive tourist trails that so many end up on, this book is for you.

The many suggestions contained in this book counter-balance the charge frequently made about capital cities — that they are exceptionally expensive. Everything included here — at the time of writing — costs under £5 for adult admission and many things included are free. But bear in mind, of course, that not only are prices subject to change, but exchange rates vary also. This point is especially relevant as the Netherlands changes currency in 2002 from the guilder to the euro.

This guide clearly and concisely explains when, where

and how you can visit a wealth of attractions in Amsterdam very cheaply and answers questions such as 'Do you have to turn up early to get an acceptable view?', 'Does something cost £5 only at a certain time?', 'Do you have to apply first for tickets?'

Splashing out for expensive admission tickets to a well-known tourist attraction is no guarantee of satisfaction. How often have you paid a visit to one of a city's most popular tourist attractions, at considerable expense, and discovered that there seemed to be no restriction on numbers admitted, or that you were herded round like cattle, pushed onwards by the crowd if you dared pause at any of the exhibits?

It is surprising how badly designed many attractions are, the most common problems being sharp edges at toddler level around display cases, just waiting to cause an accident, and bad signposting and inadequate facilities for those in wheelchairs, those otherwise disabled or those with push-chairs. Paying a big admission charge on top of such trials hardly pacifies the harassed visitor.

Boundaries of the Book

When covering an area as big as Amsterdam it can be difficult to know where the city ends. Some people define the place by telephone code; others use postal districts or boroughs or the area within the ring road. Whatever definition you subscribe to, I trust that on the whole the entries in this book represent your idea of Amsterdam.

Geography hasn't been the only matter to cause problems during the compilation of this book. For example, £5 would buy you an afternoon of coffees or a couple of drinks in many cafés and bars, but of course it would be impractical to include them all here. Likewise, you can buy an adult cinema ticket for £5 or under at many cinemas in the city, but including them all is outside the scope of this book.

This book is primarily concerned with discovering those things you can enjoy in Amsterdam that are free or inexpensive and which are unique, rare or stand out from the crowd.

That is why more theatres are included than cinemas, for example. Venues where you can enjoy a good theatrical performance for less than £5 an adult ticket are rare; cinemas showing the same old Hollywood fare are not.

A Few More Points About This Book

The book is arranged alphabetically by subject but there is also a regional index so you can easily plan a visit to a number of attractions when going to a particular area.

Every endeavour has been made to ensure details were correct when going to press. Nevertheless, obviously policies, prices and exchange rates change, so check details such as opening times and admission charges before setting out. Many places may be closed or alter opening times on particular days, especially around Christmas and on bank holidays.

Some of the places listed are administered by trusts, charities and associations that do not charge admission fees, but where a voluntary donation would be very welcome to help keep the establishment open to the public.

When visiting open spaces and nature reserves, visitors should keep to any marked paths to avoid causing any damage or disturbance.

The 020 telephone code for Amsterdam has been omitted to reduce repetition, although the area codes for other districts are included.

Some attractions and sights are mentioned more than

once. This is for ease of use, where the entry fits more than one section of the book.

Any comments or suggestions of things to include in future editions of this book would be particularly welcomed. Please write to: Ben West, *Fun For A Fiver in Amsterdam*, Pan Macmillan, 20 New Wharf Road, London N1 9RR.

The Netherlands

It's puzzling how Holland, or to use its correct name, the Netherlands, is so often overlooked as a holiday destination. Comparatively few Britons visit this flat, fertile land which is famous for windmills, clogs, tulips, canals and a particularly liberal attitude. It's a pity as the Dutch are particularly welcoming. Also, since the opening of the Channel Tunnel and the recent introduction of ferry services that have slashed sea-crossing times, the Netherlands is easier than ever to reach. Most Dutch people speak English so there's little danger of language problems. Indeed, turn on the TV and much of the time you'll see British and American programmes.

The 12 provinces of the Netherlands largely consist of lush countryside broken up by a handful of vibrant cities and some pretty towns. It must be the best country in the world for a cycling holiday. Not only is it flat, but good, safe cycle paths are plentiful in both town and country, often with dedicated traffic lights and road signs. At over 300 railway stations you can take your bike on a train. You can also hire bikes – and child seats – at many railway stations and even arrange to have your luggage sent on ahead. It's also great for a motoring holiday. The roads are good and the cities, towns and villages are all easy to reach.

If you want to see the country by train, there are lots of options from the lines fanning out from Amsterdam's Centraal Station. In often under an hour you can be by the sea, walking through the dunes, or visiting attractive towns such as Haarlem, Delft and Leiden, bustling cities like Rotterdam and Den Haag, or old fishing villages by the IJsselmeer.

One great pleasure of the Netherlands is discovering the wonderful old bars and cafés where, unlike in Britain, you are assured a decent coffee and can sample some Dutch drinks, including *jenever*, Dutch gin. You can also try the Dutch cuisine. The national dishes are seldom very adventurous – chips smothered with mayonnaise is hardly a culinary revelation – but there are some delicious Dutch staples. Some are described in the 'Restaurants, Food Cafés, Tea Rooms and Other Eateries' section of the book.

Amsterdam

Amsterdam, the capital of the Netherlands and its largest city, is a beautiful, romantic place that is small enough to explore by foot and compact enough not to overwhelm the visitor. Everything seems to have been built on a human scale. With a huge concentration of attractive historic buildings, including some of the finest 17th- and 18th-century architecture Europe has to offer, it can seem almost like something out of a fairy tale. But although Amsterdam is the capital, Den Haag (The Haag) is where the government is situated, the place the Queen lives and where the country's law courts are.

Amsterdam began as a small fishing village on marshland at the mouth of the Amstel river. Flooding was averted by dykes and polders, and today the city is saved from frequent flooding through robust land reclamation and sea defences. The township expanded quickly and became northern Europe's chief trading city. By the 17th century it was the centre of a huge empire reaching the four corners of the world, but increasing domestic unrest and constraints under Napoleonic rule prompted an erosion of the city's influence.

Amsterdam shares a number of similarities with Venice. Not only was it built on water like Venice, but in the Europe of the 17th century only these two cities could be described as truly independent. Also like Venice, in a monarchial Europe it was the capital of a republic, controlled by a Roman Catholic aristocratic elite, balanced by a strong Protestant upper middle class.

Although it has an excellently preserved historical centre, Amsterdam also manages to have at the same time the buzz of a modern, cosmopolitan city. It has a cosy ambiance, a convivial feeling the Dutch call *gezelligheid*.

Amsterdam has a lively arts scene, a fabulous range of bars and cafés, fantastic museums and an exciting nightlife. Food lovers are well catered for in the many inexpensive eateries and there are innovative shops and plenty of markets. The city is traditionally associated with liberty and tolerance, especially of religion, philosophy and politics. This has helped to put it at the cutting edge of cultural, social and economic development, bringing people and ideas together. It is also a comparatively safe place, with few of the race relations, urban sprawl and poverty problems that engulf so many other cities. Despite sex and drugs being more accessible than in most places, violent crime is surprisingly rare.

The central part of Amsterdam, the old city, occupies little more than two and a half square miles and is laid out over a series of concentric canals resembling a giant fingerprint. This network of 150 canals is spanned by more than 1,200 bridges and there are 90 islands. Unsurprisingly, one of the most attractive ways of viewing the city is on a canal boat tour.

Yet it is also a great city to walk through and takes little more than half an hour to cross on foot. Bicycles are cheap to hire and plentiful, and a big network of trams criss-cross the city. Every few doors there's an inviting café to rest at.

Amsterdam is not a city for the car. Taxis are certainly not cheap and if you drive your own car, parking is expensive, parking fines are exorbitant and orientation can be difficult.

In summer, Amsterdam is transformed into a café society, with endless tables and chairs sprawling from the cafés, bars and restaurants and along the canals. The sun lures many to the numerous open spaces, such as the centrally located Vondelpark.

At night, unlike many cities, Amsterdam's 800,000 residents don't disappear to the suburbs, leaving a dead ghost town. Instead it lights up with glowing windows and lots of lightbulbs beautifully illuminating the canal bridges.

The people of Amsterdam are very friendly, even though they receive over 1.5 million visitors annually. They're helpful, and often happy to take you to the museum you asked directions for, not just tell you where it is. They also could not be accused of being shy. They don't like curtains in their windows, and day or night do not object to people looking in. The logical extension of this, of course, is the series of windows in the red light district where you're invited to look in, to see women, and sometimes men, in their undies.

Amsterdam is a city of baffling contradictions: respectable and sleazy, old and new, traditional and alternative. It has museums dedicated to, among other things, sex, torture, cannabis and trams. Alternative culture thrives here: in fact it is an alternative destination, with bicycles for getting around, canals for roads, and cafés for smoking cannabis rather than for drinking. It's completely bizarre. Visit Amsterdam and you enter a world where you get the most sleazy, dodgy commercial enterprises ever thought up by man rubbing shoulders with beautiful monuments and historic buildings; cute kids' clothes shops sharing street space with clubs where in dark rooms you can be flogged stupid and more by a complete stranger while you're legally tripping the light fantastic; where an official drugs advice team trawls the nightclubs, happy to check your drugs for purity; where shops specialise in selling water, toothbrushes, condoms, coffins and a host of other things; where there are scores of legally trading outlets that cannot only sell you marijuana but magic mushrooms, opium seeds and more.

In a word, Amsterdam is unforgettable.

Suggestions

Here are some ideas to fill your days and nights in Amsterdam:

• stroll beside a canal, especially at sunset • take a boat tour • browse at a market • settle down for a chat in a brown café • dance the night away in a club • hire a waterbike for an hour • visit one of the 'Big Three' art collections (Rijksmuseum, Van Gogh Museum and the Stedelijk Museum of Modern Art) or one of many small art galleries • visit one of the huge variety of museums • have an evening drink in a bar on a canal-side terrace • sample the Dutch cuisine or a whole range of ethnic options • drop into a bar for some live music • experience a church classical music recital • window-shop at the endless little shops and boutiques • explore the *hofjes*, or almshouses, and secluded courtyards dotted around the city • take a cheap tour on a tram • admire a few of the approximately 7,000 historical monuments in the city centre • wander around the red light district • take a restful stroll in the leafy Jordaan district • search out the striking modern architecture or the beautiful gabled houses from Amsterdam's Golden Age • hire a bike • wander past the colourful blooms at the floating flower market.

Amsterdam's Districts

Amsterdam can be separated into a number of districts, including the following ones in the centre. The exact borders of each region are often disputed but are roughly as follows.

THE CENTRE

With the harbour behind Centraal Station at its north, the centre lies roughly between the Jordaan in the west, Plantage in the east and the Museum Quarter and the Pijp in the south. It includes the Oude Zijde (Old Side) on the eastern half and Nieuwe Zijde (New Side) on the west, which make up the two halves of medieval Amsterdam. It also encompasses the Grachtengordel (Canal Ring), which retains many impressive buildings from Amsterdam's Golden Age.

The centre is where the biggest extremes that Amsterdam has to offer lie. It contains the seedy red light district and well-worn tatty tourist trails graced with ugly *bureau de change* kiosks, cafés and souvenir shops as well as medieval churches and monuments and stunningly beautiful canal-side houses. It is rich in bars, cafés, restaurants, nightclubs, theatres and shops and has a number of squares, some with markets offering great bargains.

The centre encompasses sections of the major canals: the Herengracht, the city's grandest canal; the Prinsengracht, Amsterdam's longest 17th-century canal; and the Keizersgracht, the third of these elegant canals which follow the line of the Singel, which was the original medieval moat of the city.

The oldest church in the city, the Oude Kerk (Old Church) was built in the heart of the Old Side and today, rather bizarrely, is in the heart of the red light district, with its barely clad prostitutes touting for business at their windows. The Old Side has several museums and churches as well as a number of notable historic buildings and monuments. The New Side also boasts several museums, churches, historic buildings and monuments including the stately Koninklijk Paleis, originally the town hall and the Nieuwe Kerk (New Church), which is not all that new, as it dates from the 14th century.

THE JORDAAN

This area lies within the borders made up by four canals to the west of the city centre: the Brouwersgracht, Prinsengracht, Lijnbaansgracht and Leidsegracht.

Though just a short walk from the well-worn tourist tracks, the Jordaan is a relatively little visited delightful maze of canals and backstreets. It is village Amsterdam, leafy and tranquil with narrow, pretty canals lined with picturesque houseboats, antique shops, art galleries, welcoming cafés and smokey brown bars. Many of its restaurants now typically serve trendy world cuisine rather than the traditional Dutch food.

The name probably comes from the French word *jardin*, harking back to the time when the area was a market garden outside the walls of the city and settled by French Huguenots. It has a number of canals with botanical names, including Palmgracht, Rozengracht and Bloemgracht.

The Jordaan originated in the 17th century as a working-class district and a hundred years ago it was an overcrowded slum. But after World War II it began to attract a bohemian mix of artists, writers, students and young professionals – the sort of people who live in the Jordaan today, occupying old brewery warehouses converted to swanky apartments, pretty gabled houses and dinky little houseboats.

A walk along Bloemgracht, Egelantiersgracht or Prinsengracht is to be recommended and look out for the little *hofjes* (courtyards) along the latter. The Jordaan is less interesting south of the Rozengracht.

THE PIJP

This area is broadly bordered by Boerenwetering in the west, Singelgracht in the north, the Amstel in the east and the Amstelkanaal in the south, with Sarphatipark at its centre.

It is a large island connected to the city by 16 bridges and features straight, narrow streets, built in the 19th century to house Amsterdam's working class which was fast expanding.

The Pijp is a real melting pot of nationalities as well as being very popular with students, young couples and gays. At its core is the Albert Cuyp market, Amsterdam's biggest and busiest market, helping to keep the Pijp Amsterdam's most vibrant neighbourhood.

PLANTAGE

This is the area broadly around Plantage Doklaan, Plantage Muidergracht and Plantage Parklaan. Known as 'the plantation', in the 17th century it was chiefly parkland used by wealthy citizens in their leisure time. In the 19th century, it attracted many rich Jews who had enjoyed success in the diamond-cutting industry, and its tree-lined streets and imposing villas mean that it remains today a much sought-after residential area. It houses Amsterdam's zoo, Artis, and also the delightful Hortus Botanicus botanical garden as well as a couple of museums.

MUSEUM QUARTER

This is bordered in the north by the Rijksmuseum and Vondelpark, down Emmastraat to its southern border at about Reijnier Vinkeleskade and up Hobbemakade back to the Rijksmuseum.

It was developed in the 19th century and contains some of Amsterdam's finest museums – the massive Rijksmuseum, the Van Gogh Museum and the Stedelijk. This area has a great many galleries and art and antique dealers. There are exclusive shopping streets such as PC Hooftstraat and Van Baerlestraat as well as mansions sporting art deco gateways.

Practicalities

Travel Formalities

Citizens of nearly all European countries do not require a
visa for a stay of up to three months. A valid passport will
suffice. For further details, contact the Royal Netherlands
Embassy, 38 Hyde Park Gate, London SW7 5DP (0891 711
217).

Currency

From 2002 the Dutch guilder and florin will have been
phased out to be replaced by the euro. All prices quoted in
this book are in both guilders and euros. When the change
comes, inevitably there will be more price changes than
would normally be expected as the Netherlands adjusts to
its new currency. The published prices are a guide only.
At the time of going to press the rate was around 3.50
guilders/1.66 euros to the pound.

Currency Exchange

There are many exchange bureaus throughout the country but rates of commission can vary considerably, so make sure you agree on any charges beforehand. The most expensive are usually the private exchange booths in the tourist areas.

Tourist Information

VVV: The Amsterdam Tourist Office Stationsplein 10, opposite Centraal Station, corner of Leidseplein/Leidsestraat (0900 400 4040, Mon–Fri 0900–1700, and from outside the Netherlands +31 20 551 2525) *Open daily 0900–1700*. The English-speaking staff here can provide leaflets and maps, brochures and information about walks and cycle routes, canal trips, theatre and concert tickets, public transport tickets and telephone cards. They also help with information on transport, events, exhibitions, shows and trips outside the city. They can change money and book accommodation. The office gets very busy and there can be lengthy queues at times. There are also branches of the VVV at Centraal Station, inside the station at Platform 2 (*spoor 2*) *Open Mon–Sat 0800–1945; Sun 0900–1700*. Van Tuyll van Serooskerkenweg 125, Stadionplein *Open daily 0900–1700*. Often the latter is a lot quieter than the other offices and is convenient if you are arriving by car from the south. The VVV's monthly magazine *What's On In Amsterdam*, available from the Amsterdam Tourist Office, bookshops and hotels, contains details of theatre shows, exhibitions and many other events. Price f4.50/E2.

Holland Tourist Information Schiphol Airport
Open daily 0700–2200.

The Netherlands Board of Tourism PO Box 30783, London WC2B
6DH (dialling from UK: 020 7539 7950, www.holland.com/uk)
Provides brochures and other information.

Amsterdam Uitburo (AUB) Leidseplein 26 (0900 01 91)
Open Fri–Wed 1000–1800; Thur 1000–2100. The AUB can
help with information on the arts. It has tickets for film,
theatre, concerts and museums, including FREE events.
There are lots of FREE brochures and magazines.

Dutch Automobile Association ANWB, at Museumplein 5
Provides FREE and cheap maps, pamphlets and brochures.

City Hall Information Centre Amstel 1 (624 1111)
Has leaflets and booklets on many aspects of the city.

Public Transport

Because Amsterdam is compact, unless you are pressed for
time you may not need to budget for transport. But there
is ample choice if you do. An extensive network of trams
(17 routes) covers much of the city, with trams arriving at
stops typically every five to ten minutes. Some tram stops
have electronic indicators telling you the minute the next
trams are arriving. More than 30 bus routes serve more
outlying areas and the few places that the trams do not
reach. Nine night bus routes run long after other services
have stopped. And Amsterdam's three Metro lines serve the
suburbs and the south-eastern business districts. National
public transport information is available on 0900 9292.

To use the Metro, trams and buses you buy tickets in strips (*strippenkaarten*) starting at f3/E1.35 for two. You stamp these on boarding a bus or tram, or at a Metro station. Some trams have a conductor, who will stamp the ticket for you. Tickets are valid for an hour, even if you transfer to another bus or tram.

Tickets can be bought at GVB public transport offices, including those at Stationplein 15, Prins Hendrikkade 108 and Amstel Railway Station, Julianaplein. Tickets are also available from train stations, post offices, and many newsagents and tobacconists. Discounted daily and weekly passes valid for all forms of public transport are available.

Another option is to buy an f12/E5.40 day ticket (*dagkaart*) from a bus or tram driver, which is valid on buses, trams and the Metro for the day. You can also buy a weekly season ticket (*sterabonnement*), which for central Amsterdam costs f18/E8.10. These are available from branches of the GVB (www.gvb.nl), post offices, newsagents and tobacconists.

For many visitors to the city the best pass to buy is the Circle Tram (number 20) ticket. This tram begins and ends its journey at Centraal Station and rattles around the city passing many museums, churches, bridges and canals. It runs every ten minutes or so daily from 0900 to 1900 in both directions. Tickets are available from the Tourist Information Board, GVB branches, some hotels and on the tram itself. A one-day pass costs f12/E5.40.

Taxis are comparatively expensive in Amsterdam, but you can pick them up at ranks all over town, on the street as long as its 'taxi' sign is illuminated, or you can order one by phone through Taxicentrale, Wisseloordplein 2 (677 7777).

Electricity

Power is 220 volts, compatible with British equipment, but the Netherlands uses two-pin continental plugs so an adaptor is necessary. American visitors may need to use a transformer or convert their equipment. Hotels may have a 110/120 volt shaver outlet.

Time Zone

The Netherlands is in the Central European Time Zone, an hour ahead of Greenwich Mean Time.

Telephone

Phonecards are available from post offices, train station counters, VVV tourist offices and tobacco shops. The Amsterdam seven-figure telephone numbers shown in this book do not include the Amsterdam code, which is 020. If you are telephoning within the Netherlands but outside Amsterdam you first have to dial 020 for Amsterdam before dialling the seven-digit local number.

When calling the Netherlands from the UK dial 00 (international access code), then the Dutch country code 31, then the area code, but omitting the first 'o' (therefore 20 for Amsterdam), then the seven-figure number. 0800 (freephone) and 0900 (premium rate) numbers cannot be dialled from abroad.

When calling the UK from the Netherlands dial 00 44 plus the number, dropping the first 'o' from the area code.

SOME AREA CODES

Alkmaar – 072
Amsterdam – 020
Delft – 015
Den Haag – 070
Haarlem – 023
IJmuiden – 0255
Leiden – 071
Maastrict – 043
Rotterdam – 010
Utrecht – 030
Zaandam – 075

USEFUL NUMBERS WITHIN THE NETHERLANDS

National Directory Enquiries – 0900 8008
International Directory Enquiries – 0900 8418
Local Operator – 0800 0101
International Operator – 0800 0410

Disabled Travellers

More and more tourist and recreational enterprises are catering to the needs of disabled travellers and many public buildings are now more easily accessible. However, many hotels are in old buildings and these may have steep stairs and no lift.

Metro stations have lifts and many trains have wheelchair access. Disabled people get a discount on public transport and and usually parking is free of charge. The VVV Tourist Information Offices can give further advice. Here are some useful organisations.

Nederlands Instituut voor Zorg and Welzijn (NIZW) Postbus 19152, 3501 DD Utrecht (0 30 230 6603) Disabled access database.

Mobility International Nederland Heidestein 7, 3971 ND Driebergen (0 343 521 795) Advice on accommodation for the disabled.

Stichting Recreatie Gehandicapten Boedapeststraat 25, Hoofddorp, Postbus 4140, 2003 EC Haarlem (0 23 536 8409) Organises trips for disabled people.

Gaiskamp (633 3943) Wheelchair taxi service in operation daily between 0700–2400.

Beumer de Jong Haarlemmermeerstraat 49–53, 1058 JP Amsterdam (615 7188) Hires out wheelchairs in Amsterdam.

The Royal Association for Disability and Rehabilitation (RADAR) 12 City Forum, 250 City Road, London EC1V 8AF (020 7250 3222, www.radar.org.uk) Can give advice and has a guide to European travel for the disabled.

Health

The Netherlands has reciprocal health arrangements with other EU countries, and you require an E111 form, available from post offices. You may have to pay on the spot but can claim all or most of the costs back. There are no compulsory vaccinations unless you have travelled through a yellow fever area. See a *drogist* (chemist) or *apotheek* (pharmacy) for minor health problems. For more serious health concerns, go to the accident and emergency department of a *ziekenhuis* (hospital). Alternatively telephone the 24-hour Centrale Doktersdienst central medical service (0900 503 2042/592 3434), which can refer you to a doctor, dentist or pharmacist. Or ring the 24-hour Tourist Medical Service on 592 3355.

Hospitals with Accident and Emergency Services

Academisch Medisch Centrum Meibergdreef 9, Bilmer (566 9111/ 566 3333)

Andreas Ziekenhuis Theophile de Bockstraat 8 (511 1115)

Boven IJ Ziekenhuis Statenjachtstraat 1 (634 6346) Located in the north of Amsterdam.

VU Academisch Ziekenhuis De Boelelaan 1117 (444 4444/444 3636)

Sint Lucas Andreas Ziekenhuis Jan Tooropstraat 164 (510 8911) Located in the western suburbs.

Onze Lieve Vrouwe Gasthuis Le Oosterparkstraat 279 (599 9111) A central hospital at Oosterpark near the Tropenmuseum.

Slotervaart Ziekenhuis Louwesweg 6 (512 9333) In the south-western outskirts of the city.

Emergency Telephone Numbers

Police, Ambulance, Fire Brigade – 112

Amsterdam Main Police Station Elandsgracht 117 (559 9111)

Public Holidays

New Year's Day, Good Friday, Easter Sunday, Easter Monday, Queen's Day (30 April), Ascension Day, Whit Sunday, Whit Monday, Christmas Day, Boxing Day.

Religious Services in English

PROTESTANT

English Reform and Scottish Presbyterian Church Begijnhof 48 (624 9665) Services Sunday 1030.

Anglican Church Groenburgwal 42 (624 8877) Services Sunday 1030, 1930.

ROMAN CATHOLIC

St John and St Ursula Church, Begijnhof 30 (622 1918) Mass Sunday 1215.

JEWISH

Liberal Jewish Community Jacob Soetendorpstraat 8 (642 3562)

Orthodox Community Van der Boechorstraat 26 (646 0046)

MUSLIM

THAIBA Islamic Cultural Centre Kraaiennest 125 (698 2526)

Websites

www.amsterdam.nl Sections on both visiting and living in the city, maps, arts and culture, sports, heritage.

www.amsterdamhotspots.nl Clubs, coffeeshops, museums and other listings, events, tips, webcams of the city.

www.amsterdamlive.nl In Dutch, but there are webcams and links to other sites.

www.channels.nl Virtual tour with over 800 reviews of galleries, bars, hotels, restaurants, clubs.

www.holland.com/uk British-based Netherlands Tourist Board site covering Amsterdam, other cities, motoring, cutural Holland.

www.noord-holland-tourist.nl Lots of information about the province of North Holland, which Amsterdam is within.

www.pscw.uva.nl/sociosite/Amsterdam 'Amsterdam by bite', with lots of information and listings on all aspects of the city.

www.visitamsterdam.nl Tourist board site with city guide, on-line hotel reservations, current events and more.

A–Z Listing

Accommodation

Obviously, there can't be many options accommodation-wise in a book with a financial limit of £5. Hostels around Amsterdam fall just outside this budget. Yet there are some possibilities, although you are restricted to camping or staying in a basic cabin. There is a small extra charge for cars.

Camping Amsterdamse Bos Kleine Noorddijk 1 (641 6868) *Open Apr–Sept.* Situated in this huge expanse of woodland, camping with a tent and renting a cabin starts at around f15/E6.75.

Camping Vliegenbos Meeuwenlaan 138 (636 8855) *Open Apr–Sept. Camping with a tent is around f15/E6.75 per person.* This site in Amsterdam North is popular with younger back-packers; there are also basic cabins available to rent which can work out at around the same price if shared.

Camping Zeeburg Zuider IJdijk 20 (694 4430) *Open Mar–Dec. Camping is around f10/E4.50 per person plus f7.50/E3.40 for* *the tent.* This site is north of the centre. Cabins are also available.

Gaaspercamping Loosdrechtdreef 7 (696 7326) *Open Mar–Nov. Camping is around f15/E6.75 per person.* Site is located to the south-east of the city centre.

Almshouses (*Hofjes*)

Amsterdam's *hofjes* or almshouses are an important feature of Amsterdam, and with most being hidden away from sight off the well-worn tourist routes, they are often well worth searching out.

Most date from the 17th century and were an early form of public housing, founded by wealthy citizens to provide homes for the elderly, mostly destitute widows. The rich founders were not totally free of self-interest: they believed they would be rewarded for their Christian charity in the form of a better place in heaven, closer to God. The alms-houses originated from a wide variety of denominations including Lutheran, Reformed, Roman Catholic and Baptist. The simple houses were generally built around a central courtyard, the *hof* or garden, with a water pump situated in the centre. The elderly residents lived here for free and in the winter were given free fuel in the form of peat, but were usually expected to adhere to strict rules of conduct and were supervised by the governors of the almshouses. The Jordaan district has the biggest number of *hofjes*.

Today the almshouses are popular with both young and

old alike and there are often long waiting lists for the homes.

When you open the door through to the courtyard of one of the almshouses you enter a different world – a tranquil, green oasis far from the noisy, bustling city. The Begijnhof off the Spui is the best known of Amsterdam's more than 30 courtyards of almshouses and some, including the Begijnhof, can be visited by the public during the day for FREE on the condition that no disturbance is caused, you don't go in large groups, and that you respect the privacy of the residents.

Begijnhof Entrances at Spui 14 and Kalverstraat The Begijnhof is the Begijntjes' retreat (a religious order of unmarried women who often took vows of chastity). It is an enchanting, secluded courtyard of almshouses around a peaceful garden, built from the 14th century onwards and retains a sense of sanctity to this day. Entering the little archway on the north side of Spui Square – that so easily could be missed – the peace is surprising compared to the bustle outside. (You can also enter from touristy Kalverstraat.) It's a wonderful break from the bustling Amsterdam crowds. Rather like London's Inns of Court, it is an oasis in a time warp overlooked by the majority of visitors. The courtyard is fringed by 17th-century private houses, but there are a couple of beautiful churches which permit visitors, the Englesekerk (English Reformed Church) built in approximately 1400, and a Catholic church formed secretly from two houses in 1665 when the Roman Catholic faith was banned after the Reformation. At no. 34 is Amsterdam's oldest house, the wooden-fronted Het Houten Huis, dated 1477 (see page 44).

Claes Claeszoon Hofje 1e Egelantiersdwarsstraat 34–54, also
Eerste Egelantierstraat and Tuinstraat. Founded in 1626 by
Baptist linen merchant Claes Claeszoon Anslo, this Jordaan
complex, also known as Anslo Hofje, has three courtyards.
Most of the houses are now occupied by students of the
Sweelinck Conservatory of Music, and there is a memorial
plaque to the 17th-century organist Sweenlinck in the
Tuinstraat, with the name 'Claes Claesz. Hofje' under-
neath. In the Egelantierstraat, to the left over the door
of no. 24, there is a memorial stone bearing the Anslo
(the old name for Oslo) city arms. The entrance door
in the wall on the Eerste Egelantierdwarsstraat is usually
open.

Karthuizerhof or **Huiszitten Weduwenhof** Karthuizerstraat
21–131 This is one of Amsterdam's largest groups of almshouses and is now largely populated by young people.
Situated in the Jordaan, it has a spacious court and was
founded in 1650 to help poverty-stricken widows. It used
to consist of around 100 rooms and above the entrance to
the court are the names of the founders. The delightful
cobbled courtyard itself contains two 17th-century water
pumps with spouts in the form of dolphins, old street lamps
and pretty fenced-in lawns and flowers. Within the facade
are the arms of the city.

Lindenhofje Lindengracht 94–112 This *hofje* in the Jordaan
dates from 1614 and is the oldest surviving one.

Oudemannenhuis Oudemanhuispoort, between Oudezijds Achterburgwal and Kloveniersburgwal You can see a pair of spec-
tacles, symbolising old age, on the gateway into this alms-
house for elderly men which was built in 1754. It still

boasts an attractive 18th-century courtyard and a market for second-hand books is now in the alleyway.

Rozenhofje Rozengracht 147–181 Enter by its little ornate gates to a pretty, quiet courtyard.

St Andrieshofje Egelantiersgracht 107–114 This group of almshouses again in the Jordaan dates from 1617 and is therefore is one of the oldest in Amsterdam. A pretty blue and white tiled wall in a narrow corridor leads you into this tranquil place, founded by wealthy cattle farmer Jeff Gerritszoon to help the Roman Catholic poor. The almshouses used to have their own chapel but this is now gone. The memorial stone above the entrance to the courtyard says *Vrede Zy Met U*, peace be with you.

Suyckerhofje Lindengracht 149–163 Again in the Jordaan, this pretty *hofje* dates from 1670.

Van Brienenhofje Prinsengracht 89–133 Founder Arnout Jan van Brienen only lived long enough to see the foundation stone laid at this *hofje* which dates from 1804. A well-worn stone above the monumental gatehouse commemorates this date. The name derives from the brewery of the same name which used to be situated on the same spot.

Venetiae Elandsstraat 106–136 This Jordaan *hofje* from the mid-1600s boasts a very pretty garden.

Zevenkeurvorstenhofje Tuinstraat 197–223 This Jordaan *hofje* was founded in around 1645, but the houses now grouped around the small courtyard originate from the 18th century. The neo-Gothic chapel also situated in the courtyard dates from an even later time, 1862.

Zon's Hofje Prinsengracht 159–171 The dreary corridor opens to a beautiful, tranquil courtyard garden.

Animal Enclosures and City Farms
All are FREE.

Ridammerhoeve Amsterdamse Bos (645 5034) *Open Wed–Mon 1100–1700.* A goat farm with over 100 residents. The vast Amsterdame Bos also houses riding stables and a buffalo and bison reserve.

De Dierenpijp Lizzy Ansinghstraat 82 (664 8303) *Open daily 1100–1700.* As you approach, it seems impossible that a farm could be tucked away among the residential streets here, but calves, chickens, goats, rabbits, peacocks, sheep, a pony and aviary are all crammed in. There's also a children's playground, sand pits and a small herb garden.

De Uylenburg Staalmeesterslaan 420, Rembrandtpark (618 5235) *Open daily 0900–1700.* A small children's farm with pony rides.

Vondelpark Stadhouderskade *Open 24 hours a day.* This park in the centre of the city has an animal enclosure known as 'the petting zoo', which is home to sheep, goats, llamas and parakeets.

Annual Events

Details of many annual events are available from the Amsterdam Tourist Office (0900 400 4040/551 2525) and

Uitlijn (0900 0191). You could also visit the various websites listed in the 'Practicalities' section of the book. *What's On In Amsterdam* (f5, E2.25), available in the city, has a list of events. All events are FREE unless otherwise stated.

FEBRUARY

February Strike Commemoration Dokweker Statue, Jonas Daniel Meijerplein *Held 25 February*. A ceremony, laying a wreath at the Dockworker monument in the old Jewish quarter, to remember the anti-Nazi general strike held by dockworkers in 1941.

MARCH

Dutch literature week *Third week in March*. Various book-related events. See bookshops for details.

Blues Music Festival Meervart Theatre, Meer en Vart 1 (610 7498).

Flowers in Bloom March and April are the best times to visit the bulbfields and gardens outside Amsterdam, such as at Kenkenhof, near Lisse and around Aalsmeer.

Amsterdam Pop Prijs *Tickets cost around f15/E6.75 (420 8160, www.grap.nl)*. The finals for this local talent-spotting contest are held from March to June at different venues around the city.

Stille Omgang (Silent Procession) *Sunday in late March. Starts at Spui, passes through Kalverstraat, Nieuwendijk, Warmoes-straat, Nes and back to Spui. For information contact Gezelschap van de Stille Omgang, Zandvoortseweg 59, 2111 GS Aerdenhout*

(023 524 6229). A Catholic ceremony to commemorate the Miracle of Amsterdam in 1345, when a dying man is said to have miraculously recovered. The congregation march through the red light district, which is a sight to behold itself.

APRIL

Floriade 2002 Hoofddorp, just south-west of Amsterdam (023 562 2002) *April 1 to 15 October*. This international horticultural exhibition is only held once a decade and draws big crowds.

Rowing Races Amsterdamse Bos (646 2740) *Apr–July*. A number of rowing contests are held here through the sunnier months.

World Press Photo Oude Kerk, Oudekerksplein 23 (625 8284/676 6096, www.worldpressphoto.nl) *Apr–May. Adults f10/E4.5, concessions f7/E3.2*. This, the world's biggest photographic competition, begins its exhibition tour around the world in Amsterdam.

National Museum Weekend *Mid-April. Admission is FREE or reduced. Further information from the museums themselves or from the Amsterdam Tourist Board (0900 400 4040)*. There are lots of events at most state museums around the country. Unfortunately it means that the museums can get very crowded.

Koninginnedag (Queen's Day) *30 April*. A great time to visit the city. Amsterdam is bursting at the seams this day as thousands upon thousands of revellers have an all-day party with live music, big crowds, lots of beer and a huge free market where anyone can sell anything they like. Children are best catered for at Vondelpark, a fair is installed at Dam, while the Homomonument at Westermarkt is the centre of lesbian and gay celebrations known as the *Roze Wester* (Pink Wester), featuring live music and street dancing.

MAY

Herdenkingsdag (Remembrance Day) National Monument, Dam *4 May*. To remember those who died in World War II, there is a 30-minute service at 1930 followed by the Queen laying a wreath. After a two-minute silence military chiefs and others also lay wreaths.

Homosexual Remembrance Day Homomonument, Westermarkt *4 May*. Dutch gay organisation COC has its own ceremony to remember the homosexuals who died during World War II.

Bevrijdingsdag (Liberation Day) Vondelpark, Leidseplein, Museumplein *5 May*. To commemorate the end of German occupation in 1945, there are various events including street parties, live music, a market and political parties flogging ideology.

Oosterparkfestival Oosterpark, Oost *First week in May*. A festival with live music, food stalls, sports competitions, etc.

Luilak (Lazy Bones) *The Saturday before Whit Sunday*. If your doorbell rings at some ungodly hour, it's likely to be children observing this tradition of waking people up, as a celebration of the awakening of spring.

National Cycling Day *Second Saturday in May. For details, call* the Amsterdam Tourist Board *(0900 400 4040)*. This is cele-brated with trips along lots of special cycle routes.

Open Garden Days *For details, call the Amsterdam Tourist Board (0900 400 4040)*. The public can visit some of Amster-dam's beautiful private gardens.

National Windmill Day *Second Saturday in May. For details call Vereninging de Hollandse Molen (623 8703)*. Six working mills in Amsterdam as well as around 700 windmills and water-mills elsewhere around the country sport a blue banner to show that they are open to the public for FREE.

Dam Children's Book Market *Mid-May. Along the Dam River (627 5794)*.

EuroPerve *Last Saturday in May (620 5603)*. This event, serving the more sexually adventurous, consists of music, dancing, performances and more, with the dress code leather, latex and the like.

AIDS Memorial Day Beurs van Berlage *Last Saturday in May*. After a ceremony in which candles are lit, participants walk to Dam and release white balloons.

Kunst RAI (RAI Arts Festival) RAI Congresgebouw, Europaplein (549 1212) *From mid-May to early June*. Lots of the country's art galleries jointly exhibit the best of the contemporary art scene.

Echo Grachtenloop (Canal Run) (585 9222) *A day in late May or early June, starting at 1100. To watch is FREE, but to participate (register by 1030 at De Stadsschouwburg, Leidseplein 26) costs around f12/E5.40*. Over 4,000 people run along the

Prinsengracht and Vijzelgracht canals for a distance of about 3, 6 and 12 miles (5, 9 and 18 km).

Holland Festival *Late May through June. Various venues including the Stadsschouwburg, Leidseplein (530 7110, www. hollandfestival.nl).* Some inexpensive tickets are available for art, dance, theatre, music and operatic events. Many theatres and museums allow admission to rehearsals and there are masterclasses and back-stage tours.

JUNE

Vondelpark Openluchttheatre (Vondelpark open-air theatre) Vondelpark (523 7790) *June–Aug, Wed–Sun.* FREE live music, theatre, dance and children's shows are all performed in the park's theatre.

Amsterdam Roots Festival *(0900 0191/531 8181, www. amsterdamroots.nl)* Various venues around town are used for this established world music event, with tickets ranging from FREE to expensive.

Open Garden Days (422 1870) Owners of private gardens allow the public in to admire their horticultural achievements.

Amstel Art Book Market *Along the Amstel River. Mid-June (627 5794).*

International Theaterschool Festival Jodenbreestraat 3 and other venues around the city (527 7613, www.its.ahk.nl) *Late June. Admission ranges from about f5/E2.37 to f15/E7.11.* Students from the school perform drama, dance and cabaret.

Nieuwmarkt Antiques Market Nieuwmarkt *Open June–Sept Sun 0900–1700.*

JULY

Dam Mystery Book Market *Mid-July. Along the Dam River* (627 5794).

Julidans *Two weeks in mid-July. Various venues around Leidseplein (www.julidans.com).* An international festival of modern dance with some inexpensive tickets available.

AUGUST

Amsterdam Gay Pride Weekend (623 6565) *First weekend in August.* The highlight is the canal parade, a magnificent floating display, and there is also partying, sporting and cultural events and street performances around the city.

Theatre Parade Martin Luther Kingpark, Zuid (030 465 4577, www. mobilearts.nl) *Around the first two weeks of August daily 1500–0200. FREE until 1700, then f5/E2.25 1700–1900; f7.50/3.37 1900–2400, plus extra charges for individual shows.* An open-air circus/theatre festival with a variety of theatre, performance and music acts including ones for children in the afternoons. Over 100 artistes, more than 20 theatre tents, and several travelling restaurants all combine for this huge garden party.

Grachtenfestival (Canal Festival) (421 4542, www. grachtenfestival.nl) *Five days in mid-August.* This festival has FREE canal-side classical music concerts, often with top national and international performers. It is staged along the

Prinsengracht and Keizersgracht canals in houses, gardens and roof terraces.

Amstel Religious Book Market *Mid-August along the Amstel River (627 5794).*

Hartjesdag Zeedijk Zeedijk (625 8467) *Held on the last Monday of August.* Celebrating 'Heart Day', an old Amsterdam tradition, there is a parade of boys dressed as girls and vice versa.

Uitmarkt *Last weekend of August. Held around Leidseplein, Museumplein, Dam and Nes (www.uitmarkt.nl).* A FREE festival promoting forthcoming artistic events featuring various theatre, music, dance, cabaret and opera performances in theatres and on open-air stages in central squares around Amsterdam. Typically, previews are staged in 20-minute chunks, and the festival attracts around half a million visitors.

SEPTEMBER

Bloemen Corso (Flower Parade) *First Saturday in September (029 732 5100).* A day-long parade of floats decorated in flowers which starts at Aalsmeer ('the flower capital') at 0930 to reach the Olympic Stadium, Stadionplein at around 1300, and then onto Leidseplein, Leidsestraat, Spui and a civic reception at Dam around 1600. The parade then continues to Rembrandtplein, Vijzelstraat and Westeringschans back to Aalsmeer.

Jordaan Festival *Second week in September (626 5587).* A neighbourhood festival featuring street parties with performances by locals.

Amnesty International Film Festival De Balie, Kleine Gartman-plantsoen 10 (626 4436) *Five-day festival held only on even-numbered years.* A biennial film fest with film showings, talks and other events.

Chinatown Festival Nieuwmarkt *Held in mid-September (0900 400 4040).* Various Chinese festivities.

Monumententag (Open Monument Days) *Held second weekend in September (552 4888/626 3947, www.openmonumentendag.nl).* A nationwide event where listed historic buildings and monuments are open to the public.

OCTOBER

Children's Book Festival *Second week in October.* Bookshops celebrate children's books with various events.

High Times Cannabis Cup Melkweg, Lijnbaansgracht 234a, and all around the city (624 1777, www.hightimes.com). Various events including music and a competition to find the best cannabis.

Delta Lloyd Amsterdam Marathon *Mid-October (663 0781, www.amsterdammarathon.nl).* Around 8,000 runners and skaters follow a 21km trail twice through the city, starting and ending at the Olympic Stadium. There is also a kids' run, 10km run and a half-marathon. Near the stadium are music, dancing and various stalls.

NOVEMBER

Sinterklaas Intocht (Santa Claus Arrives) *Held in mid-November (0900 400 4040).* Many stores may start the run-up to Christmas almost the moment their summer sales end, but the

Yuletide season is officially marked in Amsterdam by this ceremony in which Sinterklaas (Santa Claus) 'arrives from Spain' by steamboat at Centraal Station. He heads a parade that includes Zwarte Pieten ('Black Peters', or black elves) from the Barbizon Palace Hotel, Prins Hendrikkade, and then moves on to Damrak, Dam, Raadhuisstraat, Rozengracht and Leidseplein.

International Documentary Filmfestival Amsterdam De Balie, Kleine Gartmanplantsoen 10 (626 1939) *Held in late November.* Film showings, discussions and other events.

DECEMBER

Winterparade Westergasfabriek, Haarlemmerweg 8–10 (681 3068) *Late December.* A short season of theatrical events.

Oudejaarsavond (New Year's Eve) *31 December.* The city is in jubilant mood, with the centre, especially Dam and Nieuwmarkt, packed with revellers.

Architecture
See also *Buildings Through the Ages* page 54.

Amsterdam is of course a delight to the eye of any visitor, but especially for lovers of architecture. There is a rich collection of 17th-century houses, with a number older than that, as well as most innovative and striking modern building designs.

The city centre is largely defined by 17th-century buildings constructed during the Netherlands' 'Golden Age'. These narrow-fronted merchants' houses are characterised by the traditionally Dutch ornamented gables. There are magnificent examples along the canals. Also, the **Westerkerk (West Church)** at Prinsengracht 279 and **Koninklijk Paleis (Royal Palace)** at Dam are particularly good examples from this era.

As in Britain, with the huge expansion of building during the later years of the Victorian age, a new period of growth occurred in Amsterdam from around 1865. The designs by architect Pierre J. H. Cuypers were dominant then and he masterminded the design of both the **Rijksmuseum** (Stadhouderskade 42) and the **Centraal Station,** which share a number of similarities.

The work of another very influential architect, H. P. Berlage, is very different from this style. He designed the **Beurs van Berlage (Stock Exchange)** at Damrak 277 and the **General Netherlands Diamond Workers' Union Building** (now the Vakbondsmuseum, Henri Polaklaan 9), which are a lot more sober and functional. The latter features a diamond-shaped pinnacle, ceramics and murals, an embellished staircase and impressive main hall.

The Scheepvaarthuis (Shipping House) on the corner of Binnenkant and Prins Hendrikkade and completed in 1916, is a very good example of the architectural style of the Amsterdam School (1912–40). Its proponents liked to make extensive use of decoration and brickwork and the Scheepvaarthuis features a number of facade sculptures and is notable for using the street layout to resemble a ship's bow. Further examples of the School are in the western and southern suburbs of the city. South of Cintuurbaan in the

Pijp is the Cooperatiehof, designed by Amsterdam School architect Piet Kramer, while there are estates by Michel de Klerk at Therese Schwartzeplein and Henriette Ronner-plein. Between Zaanstraat and Oostzaanstraat, north-west of the centre, is another of Michel de Klerk's housing estates, called **Het Schip (The Ship)** and resembling one. It was completed in 1920 and is another good example of the Amsterdam School.

Inspiring contemporary architecture has sprung up recently in the Jordaan and Nieuwmarkt districts. Theo Bosch's 1980s housing project, **the Pentagon**, is by the Zuiderkerk, St Anthoniesbreestraat, and invariably evokes a wide range of reactions. The **Ing Bank** building in the south-east of the city dates from 1987 and is interesting in that there are no right angles to its structure. The huge **Stadhuis Muziektheater** (Waterlooplein 22) courted much controversy before its opening in 1988. A number of medieval houses were demolished to make way for this new city hall and opera house, which is decked out in red brick, glass and marble.

Amstedam is dotted with interesting buildings including:

In't Aepjen (The Monkey) Zeedijk 1 *Open daily 1500–0100.* Zeedijk is the city's original dockside street. A bar is housed in this building which dates from the 16th century. The ground floor is 19th century, but the floors above show the medieval style of each wooden storey protruding out further than the one below.

20–30 Roemeer Visscherstraat Here, near Vondelpark there's an interesting row of houses dating from 1894 built in the styles of seven different countries: Germany, The Netherlands, England, France, Italy, Spain and Russia.

Het Houten Huis *Entrances at Spui 14 and Gedempte Begijnensloot.* In the tranquil Begijnhof courtyard sits Amsterdam's oldest house, the wooden-fronted Het Houten Huis, built in 1477. This, and the building at Zeedijk 1, are the only timber-fronted houses that remain in the city.

Singel Canal 140–142 The home of Banning Cocq, the main figure in Rembrandt's *Night Watch*.

Narrow houses on Singel Canal Amsterdam is known for its boasts of having the world's narrowest house, although there have long been disputes over which is the narrowest house from a choice of contenders. Property was originally taxed on frontage in Amsterdam so this encouraged a number of citizens to construct particularly narrow buildings. Singel 7 is often said to be Amsterdam's smallest house. At just one metre wide, it is also claimed by the tourist board to be the world's narrowest house. Yet what you see is in fact the rear entrance of a much larger house, so the claim is somewhat misleading. Singel 144 measures only 1.8 metres across, although it widens out inside. Singel 166 is the address of a house just 1.84 metres wide. Originally a shop was situated on the ground floor.

Oude Hoogstraat 22 This tiny house (Europe's narrowest) between the Dam and Nieuwmarkt, complete with typical Amsterdam bell-gable, is 2.02 metres wide and 6 metres deep. A textile shop is situated on the ground floor and to the right a 17th-century door leads to the Waalse Kerk (Walloon Church).

Kliene Trippenhuis (the Small Trippenhouse) Kloveniersburgwal 26 Another slim architectural example, it has a charming elevated cornice gable dating from 1696. It is 2.44 metres wide and is also known as Huis van de Koetsier van de heer Trip (Mr Trip's Coachman's House). The story goes that the Trip brothers' coachman exclaimed one day, 'Oh, if only I could be so lucky as to have a house as wide as my master's door.' His master overheard this and the coachman's wish was granted.

Trippenhuis (Trippenhouse) Kloveniersburgwal 29 This enormous house is in fact two buildings. The centre windows are false to preserve the symmetry. The Trippenhouse was built in 1660 for the wealthy Trip brothers, Lodewijk and Hendrik, who made their fortune in trading iron, copper, artillery and ammunition.

Gravenstraat Between numbers 17 and 19 Gravenstraat is what is dubbed 'the smallest shop in Europe', being 1.83 metres wide by 2 metres deep, built up against the medieval Niuwe Kerk (New Church). In addition, to both left and right of the doorway into the New Church there are two small shops, Gravenstraat 10 and Nieuwezijds Voorburgwal 125, each with floorspace dimensions of 1.6 metres by 3 metres.

Keizersgracht Canal There are some architecturally interesting buildings along the canal. At no. 123 is the 'House with the Heads', an excellent example of the Dutch Renaissance style. Apparently the chiselled heads represent classical gods, and according to folklore they are the heads of six burglars decapitated when they broke into the cellar.

Keizersgracht 174–176 Now Greenpeace's international

headquarters, this is an impressive art nouveau building designed by Gerrit van Arkels. No. 324 is the neoclassical Felix Meritis building. 'Happiness through achievement' is written over the door.

Herengracht 380–382 A unique house, having been designed in the 1880s in the early French Renaissance style of a chateau. It was also Amsterdam's first house to have electricity installed.

Herengracht The area between Leidsestraat and Vijzelstraat is known as the Golden Bend and boasts some of the biggest mansions in Amsterdam. Though the Dutch influence is there, architecturally the houses echo the Louis XIV, XV and XVI eras. No. 470 is now home of the Goethe Institut and therefore the interior can be seen.

Regulierstraat The road has a number of buildings of architectural interest including number 34, which has a huge eagle gable and an unusual twin entrance. Look out for the woodwork at no. 57 and the statue of a stork at no. 92.

Prinsengracht Notable buildings include the neoclassical Palace van Justitie (Court of Appeal) at no. 436. Originally an orphanage in 1666, it remained one until the early 19th century, by which time more than 4,000 children were packed in here. On Leidseplein at no. 25 is the Stadsschouwburg Theatre, completed in 1894 and at Marnixstraat is the art nouveau Americain Hotel, dating from 1902. No. 1047 at the corner of Reguliersgracht has a bell gable dating from c.1750 and is a five-storey building measuring just 3 metres by 3 metres.

Amstelveld Here, where the Prinsengracht meets Reguliersgracht, the timbered Amstelkerk stands. It was built in
1670 as a temporary church until the planned permanent
one was built, but it remains in use today. On the opposite
side of the canal, de Duif (the Dove) Catholic church at
no. 756 dates from 1796.

Art Galleries

There are more than 100 art galleries scattered around
Amsterdam. Some of the more established ones are to be
found along the Keizersgracht, Rokin and in the Spiegel-
wartier. Admission is FREE unless otherwise stated.

Amsterdamse Centrum voor Fotographie Bethanienstraat 9 (622
4899) *Open Wed–Sat 1200–1700, closed July.* Photographers
ranging from local through to international talents. A dark-
room is for hire.

Animation Art Berenstraat 19 (627 7600) *Open Tues–Fri
1100–1800; Sat 1100–1700; Sun 1300–1700.* Cartoons.

Annet Gelink Laurierstraat 187 (330 2066) *Open Tues–Sat
1100–1800.* Spacious contemporary gallery.

ArCam Waterlooplein 213 (620 4878, www.arcam.nl) *Open Tues–
Fri 1300–1700.* Exhibitions, tours and talks on architecture.

Arti et Amicitiae Rokin 112 (623 2092) *Open Tues–Fri
1200–1800; Sat, Sun 1200–1700.* An artists' club with contemporary art.

Art Industry Feredinand Bolstraat 1 (777 9910) *Open Wed–Sat
1100–1800.* Netherlands' contemporary works.

Art Works Herengracht 229–231 (624 1980) *Opening times vary.* European sculptures and paintings.

Aschenbach Gallery Bilderdijkstraat 165c (685 3580) *Opening times vary.* Photography and figurative works.

Atelier 408 Herengracht 408 (622 9314) *Open Thur–Sat 1230–1730 and variable opening hours Wed, Sun.* Contemporary art.

BMB Kerkstraat 127–129 (622 9963) *Open Wed–Sat 1230–1730.* Contemporary works.

Braggiotti Gallery Singel 424 (638 9654) *Open Wed–Sat 1200–1800.* Contemporary shows. Art deco-style café with art gallery.

Clement Prinsengracht 845 (625 1656) *Open Tues–Sat 1100–1730.* Specialising in prints.

Collection d'Art Keizersgracht 516 (622 1511) *Open Wed–Sat 1300–1700.* Shows the more established Dutch artists.

De Zaaier Keizersgracht 22 (420 3154) *Open daily 1030–1800.* Local artists.

Donkersloot Galerie PC Hooftstraat 127 (572 2722) *Open daily 1000–2100.* Late-opening gallery mainly showing national rather than international artists.

Frozen Fountain Prinsengracht 629 (622 9375/9675) *Open Mon 1300–1800; Tues–Fri 1000–1800; Sat 1100–1700.* A shop rather than gallery with impressive designer furnishings by the best young designers.

Galerie Akinki Lijnbaansgracht 317 (638 0480, www.akinki.nl) *Open Tues–Sat 1300–1800.* Contemporary Dutch works.

Gallery Delaive Spiegelgracht 23 (625 9087) *Open Tues—Sat 1100—1700; Sun 1200—1700.* If you're after the big names, this gallery regularly exhibits world-famous artists such as Picasso and Matisse.

Galerie van Gelder Planciusstraat 9a, Haarlemmerplein, Jordaan (627 7419) *Open Tues—Sat 1300—1730.* Installation art.

Gallery Nine Keizersgracht 570 (627 1097) *Open Wed—Sun 1300—1700.* Abstract art.

Gallery Steimer Reestraat 25 (624 4220) *Opening times vary.* Contemporary jewellery.

Glasgalerie Kuhler Prinsengracht 134 (638 0230) *Open Tues—Sat 1200—1800.* Contemporary artworks.

Go Gallery Prinsengracht 64 (422 9580, www.gogallery.nl) *Open Wed—Sat 1200—1800.* Inspired exhibitions of local works.

Guido de Spa Weteringdwarsstraat 34 (622 1528) *Open Wed—Sat 1400—1700.* Etchings, paintings and sculptures.

Hamer Leliegracht 38 (626 7394) *Open Tues—Sat 1330—1730.* Specialising in naive art.

Het Molenpad Prinsengracht 653 (625 9680) *Opening times vary.* This brown café located near lots of antique shops, has a terrace overlooking the canal and a small art gallery for local artists.

Huis Marseilles Keizergracht 401 (531 8989, www.huismarseilles.nl) *Open Tues—Sun 1100—1700. Adults f5/E2.25 concessions f2.5/ E1.15.* Photographic exhibitions.

Immaculate Conception Max Euweplein 45 (427 3716) *Open Tues—Sun 1200—1800.* Contemporary art.

Jaski Nieuwe Spiegelstraat 27–29 (620 3939) *Opening times vary. Artworks by the CoBrA movement.*

Josine Bokhoven Prinsengracht 154 (623 6598) *Open Tues–Sat 1300–1800.* Contemporary works.

Kattenkabinet Herengracht 497 (626 5378) *Opening times vary. Admission f10/E4.50.* A collection of artworks featuring cats.

Lambiek Kerkstraat 78 (626 7543) *Open Mon–Fri 1100–1800; Sat 1100–1700.* Cartoons.

Lieve Hemel Nieuwe Spiegelstraat 3 (623 0060) *Opening times vary.* Realist art.

Melkweg Lijnbaansgracht 234a (624 1777, www.melkweg.nl) *Open Wed–Sun 1400–2000.* As well as regular art exhibitions, this cultural centre has theatre, dance and music events.

Modern African Art Gallery Kerkstraat 123 (620 1958) *Open Mon–Fri 1100–1700; Sat 1100–1800.* It would be safe to assume that this gallery deals in modern African art.

Nanky de Vreeze Lange Leidsedwarsstraat 198 (627 3808) *Open Wed–Sat 1200–1800.* Contemporary art.

Oude Kerk Oudekerksplein 23 (625 8284, www.oudekerk.nl) *Open Mon–Sat 1100–1700.* As well as the prestigious World Press Photo exhibition in April or May, a very varied programme of other exhibitions are held throughout the year.

Parade Prinsengracht 799 (427 4646) *Open Mon–Sat 1100–1800.* Postmodern art.

Prestige Art Reguliersbreestraat 46 (624 0104) *Open Mon–Sat 1100–1700.* 17th- to 19th-century oils.

Ra Vijzelstraat 80 (626 5100) *Open Tues–Sat 1200–1800.* Modern jewellery.

Reflex Weteringschans 79a (627 2832, www.reflex-art.nl) *Open Tues–Sat 1100–1800.* National and international exhibitions.

SAK Keizersgracht 22 (420 3154) *Open daily 1100–1830.* Spacious gallery showing local artists.

Stedelijk Museum Bureau Rozenstraat 59 (422 0471) *Open Tues–Sun 1100–1600.* A venue often with less established contemporary Amsterdam artists.

Steendrukkerij Amsterdam Lauriergracht 80 (624 1491) *Open Wed–Sat 1300–1730.* Woodcuts and lithography.

Auctioneers

If you've just bought a so-called antique in Amsterdam, these auctioneers will value it for FREE and indicate whether you've unearthed one of Da Vinci's previously unknown masterpieces or bought a dud. An auction (most are FREE admission) can be one of the best shows in town.

Christies Cornelis Schuytstraat 57 (575 5255) *Open Mon–Fri 0900–1730.*

Sotheby's de Boelelaan 30 (550 2200) *Open Mon–Fri 0900–1700.*

Boat Tours and Rentals

With canals and bridges making up so much of Amsterdam, a boat trip is an excellent way to familiarise yourself with the city and to see the distinctive 17th-century canal-side gabled houses, built in the city's 'Golden Age'. Taking a canal boat tour may seem a naff, touristy thing to do, yet the typically hour-long tours are a great introduction to Amsterdam. Many boats depart from a variety of spots around Centraal Station and Damrak every 15 minutes or so.

Best of Holland Damrak 34 (623 1539) *Cruises depart from Rederij Lovers landing stage, opposite Centraal Station. Regular one-hour cruises start at ƒ13/E5.85 adults, ƒ6.50, E2.95 under-13s.*

Holland International Prins Hendrikkade 33a (622 7788) *Cruises depart from opposite Centraal Station. Regular one-hour cruises cost ƒ17.50/E7.90 adults, ƒ12.50/E5.65 under-13s.*

Lindbergh Damrak 26 (622 2766) *Regular one-hour cruises cost from ƒ13/E5.85 adults, ƒ8/E3.60 under-13s.*

Rederij Lovers Prins Hendrikkade (622 2181) *Cruises depart from opposite Centraal Station. Regular one-hour cruises cost from ƒ17.50/E7.90 adults, ƒ10/E4.50 under-13s.*

Rondvaarten Kooy BV Rokin (623 3810) *Regular one-hour cruises cost from ƒ13/E5.85 adults, ƒ8/E3.60 under-14s.*

OTHER CRUISES

Departures in the Centraal Station area, similar prices:

Meyer Damrak, moorings 4–5

Rederij Plas Damrak, moorings 1–3

Departures in the Rijksmuseum area:

Amsterdam Canal Cruises Nic. Witsenkade 1a

Rederij Boekel opposite Nassaukade 380 (in summer only)

Rederij Noord-Zuid Stadhouderskade 25, opposite Park Hotel

Departures in the Muntplein area:

Rederij Kooij opposite Rokin 125

WATERBIKES

Canal Bike Weteringschans 24 (626 5574) *Open Nov–Mar daily 1000–1730; Apr–Oct 1000–2200. Costs per hour are f10/E4.50 per person with three or four people sharing a pedalo, f12.50/E5.65 if one or two.* You can hire a waterbike (a pedalo to you, pal) from Canal Bike and drop it off at any of these four mooring points: Leidsekade at Leidseplein; Keizersgracht, by corner of Leidsestraat; Stadhouderskade, opposite the Rijksmuseum; and Prinsengracht by the Westerkerk and Anne Frank Huis. But beware, the waterways get alarmingly busy.

Aan de Wind Mauritskade 1 (692 9124) *Open Tues–Sun 0830–2200.* Waterbikes for similar charges to Canal Bike (above). Ask for a FREE route map.

Buildings Through the Ages

See also *Architecture*, page 41.

MEDIEVAL AMSTERDAM

Agnietenkapel Oudezijds Voorburgwal 231 Gothic chapel built 1470.

Begijnhof 34 Dating from around 1420, the city's oldest wooden house.

Oude Kerk Oudekerksplein 23 14th-century Gothic church.

Nieuwe Kerk Dam church built 1408.

Waag Nieuwemarkt 4 Originally a gateway in the city wall, built 1488.

16TH-CENTURY AMSTERDAM

In't Aepjen Zeedijk 1 A bar built in the mid-16th century with wooden storeys each of which protrude further than the one below.

Montelbaanstoren Oude Waal, Oude Schans 2 The lower part of the tower was completed in 1512 and formed part of the city's fortifications.

17TH-CENTURY AMSTERDAM

Portuguese Synagogue Mr Visserplein 3 Built 1675.

Rembrandthuis Jodenbreestraat 4 Rembrandt's home from 1639 to 1658, it was built in 1606.

Theatermuseum Herengracht 166–168 17th-century building with a splendid spiral staircase and ornate plasterwork.

Westerkerk Prinsengracht 281 Renaissance-style Dutch Protestant church built 1622.

Zuiderkerk St Antoniebreestraat 130–132 Protestant church designed by Hendrick de Keyser and completed in 1611.

18TH-CENTURY AMSTERDAM

De Gooyer windmill Funenkade 5 Corn mill dating from around 1725.

Felix Meritis Building Keizersgracht 324 Neoclassical building completed 1778.

Van Loon Museum Keizersgracht 672 Well-preserved 17th-century house with 18th-century decor.

19TH-CENTURY AMSTERDAM

Centraal Station Stationplein Grand train station completed in 1889.

Concertgebouw Concertgebouwplein 2–6 Neo-Renaissance concert hall from 1888.

Rijksmuseum Stadhouderskade 42 Neo-Gothic museum completed in 1885.

20TH-CENTURY AMSTERDAM

Tuschinskitheater Reguliersbreestraat 26–28 Built 1921, magnificent art deco blended with Amsterdam School.

Stadhuis-Musiektheater Waterlooplein 22 Many medieval houses

---

were destroyed to make way for this controversial 1988 building.

Cafés and Bars

One of Amsterdam's great pleasures is sampling its incredible array of cafés, bistros and bars. Life in the city revolves around them – they're almost communal living rooms. Amsterdam has over a thousand cafés, from the grand to the cosy and informal. Most published here are open from noon or earlier until midnight or later, unless otherwise stated.

The term 'café' has a much wider meaning in the Netherlands than in the UK. The word covers the kind of place you might have a coffee, but is nearer to being a pub or bar. Many have terraces with outdoor seating, often covered and heated in winter. Do not be confused by *Koffieshops*, which rather than specialising in selling coffee (as a *koffiehuis* would), can legally sell soft drugs (see page 81).

Cafés can be separated into different types. **Brown cafés (*bruin kroegen*)** are typical of the Netherlands and are the nearest equivalent to good British pubs. They are cosy and some are centuries-old and many have sand on the floors, wood-panelled walls worn smooth by the years, and tobacco-stained ceilings darkened by decades of cigarette smoke, which is how they got their name. Beware of newer wannabes pandering to tourists which have simply slapped on some brown paint. Brown cafés serve hot chocolate and coffee, but beer and schnapps are the most popular choices for customers. They tend to be small so even a handful of people in them can make them appear crowded, creating the convivial atmosphere they are renowned for providing. The city centre and the Jordaan district have the most authentic ones.

Grand cafés are a cross between the better Parisian cafés and Viennese coffee houses. They tend to be more expensive, but then they usually have wonderful spacious interiors to compensate. Beware of bigger pubs scattering a few comfy chairs around and calling themselves grand cafés. Many cafés, but especially grand cafés, have a table or racks with a selection of magazines and papers to read.

Proeflokalen **(tasting houses)** are bars which have existed since the 17th century and are geared to providing liqueurs, schnapps and flavoured spirits, many distilled on the spot. They serve *jenever* (Dutch gin), made from juniper berries, which is weaker and more oily than the British variety. *Jonge* (young) *jenever* is the most popular, as *oude* (old) *jenever* tastes more strongly of juniper and is more of an aquired taste. It is sometimes flavoured, with lemon and blackberries being popular additions, and is traditionally drunk chilled, in one gulp, alongside a glass of beer, which is known as *kopstoot*, or 'a kick in the head'. Originally potential customers would be given free samples before making their purchase, but today nothing's free.

Beer-tasting houses (*bierproeflokaal*) provide a wider-than-normal selection of brews. By the way, don't feel cheated when you order a beer and you get a little glass with two fingers of foam at the top. That's the way the Dutch drink their beer. Many places now allow you to order a half-litre *grote bier* (big beer), although that announces that you are a tourist.

Many cafés offer snacks or a short menu, but those that focus a bit more on food are called **eetcafés.** You can just have a drink in these.

Irish pubs have become very popular in Amsterdam in recent years. The established ones included below are a better bet than the formulaic chains springing up to cash in on the craze.

Many cafés do not fully fit into any of these categories and straddle two or three. A number of cafés and bars mentioned here could equally justify inclusion in the 'Restaurants, Food Cafés, Tea Rooms and Other Eateries' section (see page 126).

Aas van Bokalen Keizersgracht 335 (623 0917) *Open daily 1700–0100*. Pleasant brown café.

The Balmoral Nieuwe Doelenstraat 24 (554 0600) *Open Mon–Thur 1600–0100; Fri 1600–0300; Sat 1400–0300; Sun 1400–0100*. Scottish pub with live music on Wednesdays at 2100.

Bar Bep Nieuwe Zijds Voorburgwal 260 (626 5649) *Open Sun–Thur 1200–0100; Fri, Sat 1200–0300*. Hip bar with deep red walls and olive green seating.

Bar Diep Nieuwe Zijds Voorburgwal 256 (420 2020) *Open Sun–Thur 1700–0100; Fri, Sat 1700–0300*. Another trendy, wacky bar.

Belgique Gravenstraat 2 (625 1974) *Open Sun–Thur*

1200–0100; Fri, Sat 1200–0300. As the name suggests, there are Belgian beers (over 50) at this comfortable little bar.

Blarney Stone Nieuwendijk 29 (623 3830) *Open Mon–Thur 1600–0100; Fri 1600–0300; Sat 1400–0300; Sun 1400–0100.* Irish pub, unsurprisingly.

Blincker Sint Barberenstraat 7–9 (627 1938) *Open Sun–Thur 1600–0100; Fri, Sat 1600–0200.* Modern theatre café.

Brouwerij 't Ij Funenkade (622 8325) *Open Wed–Sun 1500–2000.* This friendly pub and micro-brewery located next to Amsterdam's most central windmill, the De Gooyer (dating from 1664), was previously a public bath house.

Brouwhuis Maximilliaan (Brewery House Maximillian) Kloveniersburgwal 6–8 (624 2778/626 6280) *Open Tues, Wed, Sun 1500–0100; Thur–Sat 1200–0200.* Homely brewery/pub off Nieuwmarkt Square with a restaurant, tasting room, conducted tours and beer seminars.

Café Americain Leidsekade 97 (556 3000) *Opening times vary.* A magnificent, elegant grand café dating from 1902 with art deco and art nouveau decoration. It's a great venue for breakfast, but not cheap. It has a non-smoking room, quite a rarity in Amsterdam. Below the American Hotel, it is a city landmark.

Café Chris Bloemstraat 42 (624 5942) *Open Mon–Thur 1400–0100; Fri, Sat 1400–0200.* This is one of Amsterdam's oldest and finest brown cafés, which opened in 1624 and was reputedly the drinking hole of the builders of the nearby 17th-century Westerkerk Church. On Sunday afternoons from September until March from around 1600 there are live performances of extracts from operas and operettas with a sort of opera karaoke.

Café Cox Marnixstraat 429 (620 7222) *Open Sun–Thur 1000–2230; Fri, Sat 1000–0100*. Café in the Stadsschouwburg theatre building on Leidseplein.

Café Cuba Nieuwmarkt 3 (627 4919) *Open daily 1200–0100*. A strong Cuban feel at this attractive bar.

Café de Dam Damstraat (624 5331) *Opening times vary*. Dubbed 'the smallest pub in town', this exists in what used to be the living room of a house. Consisting of five small tables; some barstools, an ornate old silver cash register and huge espresso machine, it also has a collection of British football scarves hanging from the ceiling as a nod of thanks to the large proportion of UK customers.

Café Dante Spuistraat 320 (638 8839) *Open Sun–Thur 1100–0100; Fri, Sat 1100–0300*. Art deco-style spacious café with art gallery and big choice of wines and beers.

Café Dantzig Zwanenburwal 15 (620 9039) *Open Mon–Fri 0900–0100; Sat 0900–0200; Sun 0900–2400*. A very spacious grand café with a terrace on the banks of the Amstel.

Café de Druif Rapenburgplein 83 (624 4530) *Open Sun–Thur 1100–0100; Fri, Sat 1100–0200*. A charming brown café loved by the locals which retains its old-fashioned decoration.

Café de Jaren Nieuwe Doelenstraat 20–22 (625 5771) *Open Sun–Thur 1000–0100; Fri, Sat 1000–0200*. Serving simple dishes, an ex-bank that's become a very spacious, lofty-ceilinged grand café. It has big windows and terraces on the River Amstel.

Café de Koe Marnixstraat 381 (625 4482) *Open Sun–Thur 1600–0100; Fri, Sat 1600–0300.* A noisy bar catering for a young crowd.

Café de Sluiswacht Jodenbreestraat 1 (625 7611) *Open Mon– Thur 1130–0100; Fri, Sat 1130–0300; Sun 1130–1900.* A small café near Waterlooplein with a pleasant peaceful terrace overlooking the canal. No, you're not that drunk, the building really does lean that much.

Café de Vergulde Gaper Prinsenstraat 30 (624 8975) *Open daily 1000–0100.* Ex-pharmacy transformed into a grand café with a nice terrace.

Café du New Metropolis Oosterdok 2 (531 3233) *Opening times vary.* A café with a view of the city.

Café Ebeling Overtoom 52 (689 1218) *Open Mon–Thur 1100–0100; Fri, Sat 1100–0300, Sun 1200–0100.* Easy-going café-bar in the museum quarter.

Café Hoppe Spui 18–20 (420 4420) *Open Sun–Thur 0800–0100; Fri, Sat 0800–0200.* The area around Spui Square has many brown cafés, including this, the oldest dating from 1670. It can also become one of the most crowded, after work. There's sawdust and sand on the floor, nicotine-coloured lamps, barrels set into the walls and live jazz on Monday evenings. A door behind the bar allows customers to walk to the newer bar before it closes itself by means of a sack of sand on a rope pulley.

Café Karpershoek Martelaarsgracht 2 (624 7886) *Open Mon–Sat 0700–0100; Sun 0900–0100.* A brown café dating back to 1629 with ceramics on the walls. It livens up when the local office workers appear.

Café Luxembourg Spuistraat 22–24 (620 6264) *Open Sun–Thur 0900–0100; Fri, Sat 0900–0200.* A large, atmospheric grand café overlooking Spui Square, a survivor of a bygone era with high ceilings and smart white-aproned attentive waiters. There's a reading table full of magazines and papers, pavement tables and plenty of seating inside. A popular meeting place for large groups of friends, but also popular in the day for a quiet coffee. Excellent breakfasts, and the dim sum and club sandwiches are also popular.

Café Nol Westerstraat 109 (624 5380) *Open Sun–Thur 2100–0300, Fri, Sat 2100–0400.* Check out the interior of this Jordaanese bar popular with the locals where each night from about 2100 until late, there's FREE music – accordion music, yodelling, oompah ballads and a gigantic singalong of old Amsterdam songs at this sort of working man's club of the Jordaan.

Café Papeneiland Prinsengracht 2 (624 1989) *Opening times vary.* This was established by a coffin-maker in 1642, who also sold beer. The name means Papists' Island and a tunnel once ran from the café as an escape route for Catholics during the Reformation. A very apppealing brown café on the canal bank with an ancient stove, Delft tiles and panelled walls, it's straight out of a Rembrandt picture. It is by the junction of Prinsengracht and the pretty Brouwersgracht canal.

Café Schiller Rembrandtplein 26 (624 9846) *Open Sun–Thur 1600–0100; Fri, Sat 1600–0200*. Although located in the middle of one of Amsterdam's most tackily touristy areas, this dimly lit café is largely populated by locals. For many years this café, owned by hotelier and painter Frits Schiller, was the meeting place for the city's bohemian contingent and his paintings of Dutch actors and cabaret artists still feature here along with the original art deco fittings.

Café Tabac Brouwersgracht 101 (622 6520) *Open Mon 1000–1800; Tues–Thur, Sun 1100–0100; Fri, Sat 1100–0300*. Laid-back brown café in the Jordaan.

Café Ter Kuile Torensteeg 6 (639 1055) *Opening times vary*. A café with a terrace on the canal bridge.

Café 't Monumentje Westerstraat 120 (624 3541) *Open Mon–Thur 0830–0100; Fri, Sat 0830–0300; Sun 1100–0100*. Little brown café in the Jordaan.

Café 't Smalle Egelantiersgracht 12 (623 9617) *Open Sun–Thur 1000–0100; Fri, Sat 1000–0200*. A quaint brown café in the Jordaan neighbourhood, the most rewarding area if you are in search of them. This one opened in 1786 as a gin distillery. Restored in the 1970s with features including old porcelain beer pumps, it has a small, pleasant canal-side terrace.

Cul-de-Sac Oudezijds Achterburgwal 99 (625 4548) *Opening times vary*. An ever-popular brown bar serving good food.

De Admiraal Herengracht 563 (626 2150) *Open Mon–Sat 1630–2300*. A brown café resembling a distillery.

De Balie Kliene Gartmanplantsoen 10 (553 5130, www.balie.nl) *Open Sun–Thur 1000–0100; Fri, Sat 1000–0200.* Popular café at Leidseplein.

De Beiaard Spui 30 (622 5110) *Open Sun–Thur 1200–0100; Fri, Sat 1200–0200.* A convivial bar with a pleasant conservatory and a wide variety of beers, some on draught.

De Bierkoning Paleisstraat 125 (625 2336) *Opening times vary.* A beer bar of note.

De Brakke Grond Nes 43 (626 0044) *Open daily 1100–0100.* Within the Flemish Cultural Centre, there is a good selection of Belgian beers.

De Buurvrouw St Pieterpoortsteeg 29 (625 9654) *Open Sun– Thur 2000–0200, Fri, Sat 2000–0300.* With endless loud music, don't come to this bar for a quiet drink.

De Doffer Runstraat 12–14 (622 6686) *Opening times vary.* Bar popular with students.

De Drie Fleschjes Gravenstraat 18 (624 8443) *Open Mon–Sat 1200–2030; Sun 1500–1900.* This tasting house, 'The Three Bottles', dates from 1650 and has rows of old wooden casks running its length. Unfortunately, at times it can get rows of tourists too. There is a display case containing *kalkoentjes*, little bottles with painings of ex-mayors of the city upon them.

De Duivel Regulierswarsstraat 87 (626 6184, www.deduivel.nl) *Open Sun–Thur 2000–0200; Fri, Sat 2000–0300.* Hip bar near Rembrandtplein.

De Engelbewaarder Kloveniersburgwal 59 (625 3772) *Open*

Mon—Sat 1200—0100; Sun 1400—0100. A quiet café with a good choice of beers and live jazz on Sunday afternoons.

De Fles Vijzelstraat 137 (624 9644) *Opening times vary*. Brown café that does good food.

De Hoogte Nieuwe Hoogstraat 2a (626 0604) *Open Mon—Thur 1000—0100; Fri, Sat 1000—0300; Sun 1200—0100*. Popular bar catering for a younger crowd.

De IJsbreker Weesperzijde 23 (665 3014) *Opening times vary*. Popular café with a terrace on the banks of the Amstel.

De Kroon Rembrandtplein 17 (625 2011) *Open Sun—Thur 1000—0100; Fri, Sat 1000—0200*. A grand café whose neo-colonial decor of wood and chandeliers injects some refinement into the Rembrandtplein. Its galleried bar was a meeting place for 19th-century artists and upon the walls hang glass cases displaying monkey skeletons, insects, snake skins and the like. It attracts a varied crowd of all ages. It is located in a building housing radio and TV studios so you may find yourself standing next to a Dutch TV celeb. Then again, if you don't live in the Netherlands, you're not likely to know, are you? There's a good view of Rembrandtplein from the balcony.

De Kuil Oudebrugsteeg 27 (623 4848) *Open Sun—Thur 1200—2400; Fri 1200—0100; Sat 1200—0300*. Pleasantly straddles the gap between brown café and coffee shop.

De Ooievaar St Olofspoort 1 (420 8004) *Open daily 1300—0100*. A long-established *proeflokaal* with a good choice of drinks.

De Pieper Prinsengracht 424 (626 4775) If you want the brown café experience, come here. You can get a decent Dutch pub lunch at this 331-year-old, small well-located brown café at the corner of Prinsengracht and Leidsegracht. Impressive stained-glass windows provide a picturesque view of the two canals.

De Prins Prinsengracht 124 (624 9382) *Open Sun–Thur 1000–0100; Fri, Sat 1000–0200.* A brown café overlooking Westerkerk and the Anne Frank Huis.

De II Prinsen Prinsenstraat 27 (624 9722) *Open Sun–Thur 1000–0100; Fri, Sat 1000–0300.* An airy café with a spacious terrace, big light windows and a mosaic floor.

De Reiger Nieuwe Leliestraat 34 (624 7426) *Open Sun–Thur 1100–0100; Fri, Sat 1200–0100.* A pleasant brown bar and bistro in a tranquil street.

De Schutter Voetboogstraat 13–15 (622 4608) *Open Sun– Thur 1100–0100; Fri, Sat 1100–0200.* A good-value *eetcafé/ bierproeflokaal.*

De Smoeshaan Theater Bellevue, Leidsekade 90 (625 0368) *Opening times vary.* Popular theatre café.

De Still Spuistraat 326 (620 1349) *Open Mon–Thur 1530–0100; Fri–Sun 1300–0100.* More than 420 whiskies to choose from.

De Tuin Tweede Tuinswarsstraat 13 (624 4559) *Open Mon–Thur 1000–0100; Fri, Sat 1000–0200; Sun 1100–0100.* A brown café in the Jordaan with a good selection of beers.

De Twee Zwaantjes Prinsengracht 114 (625 2729) *Open Sun– Thur 1000–0100; Fri, Sat 1000–0200.* This pleasant café decorated with stained glass has regular live music evenings on Fridays, Saturdays and Sundays.

De Zotte Raamstraat 29 (626 8694) *Open Sun–Thur 1700–0100; Fri, Sat 1700–0300.* Good food and big choice of beers.

Dubliner Dusartstraat 51, De Pijp (679 9743) *Opening times vary.* The oldest Irish pub in Amsterdam.

Du Lac Haarlemmerstraat 118 (624 4265) *Open Sun–Thur 1600–0100; Fri, Sat 1600–0300.* Bright and brash grand café with conservatory and gallery.

Durty Nelly's Warmoesstraat 117 (638 0125) *Opening times vary.* One of the rash of Irish pubs in Amsterdam, this one is in the red light district.

Eetcafé Loetfe Johannes Vermeerstraat 52 (662 8173) *Open Mon–Fri 1100–0100; Sat 1730–0100.* A bar serving meals from f10/E4.50.

Eik en Linde Plantage Middenlaan 22 (622 5716) *Open Mon–Fri 1100–0100; Sat 1100–0200; Sun 1400–0100.* A brown café off the tourist track near Artis with a billiard table in the centre and mementoes on the walls.

Felix Meritis Café Keizersgracht 324 (626 2321) *Open Mon–Fri 0900–1900.* A popular, attractive theatre café.

Finch Noordermarkt 5 (626 2461) *Open Mon 1800–0100; Tues–Thur, Sun 1100–0100; Fri, Sat 1100–0300.* Trendy bar in an attractive square.

Flying Dutchman Martelaargracht 13 (622 1076) *Open Mon–Sat 1200–0100; Sun 1400–0100.* A popular bar.

Gasthuys Grimburgwal 7 (622 8230) *Opening times vary.* A long, narrow brown café popular with university students, with bank notes from all over the world hanging from the ceiling.

Gollem Raamsteeg 4 (626 6645) *Opening times vary.* A beer café north of Spui Square with around 200 brews as well as live music on Friday evenings.

Grand Café Heineken Hoek Kleine Gartmanplantsoen 1–3 (623 0700) *Opening times vary.* International cuisine as well as a popular drinking den.

Grand Café Raffles Kleine Gartmaplantsoen 5 (638 7220) *Open Sun–Thur 0900–0100; Fri, Sat 0900–0300.* Swish grand café on Leidseplein.

Hard Rock Café Korte Leidsedwarsstraat 28–32 (523 7625) *Open Sun–Thur 1100–0100; Fri, Sat 1100–0300.* The food is bad value but as elsewhere it's geared to the rock fan.

Henri Prouvin Gravenstraat 20 (623 9333) *Open Tues–Fri 1500–2300; Sat 1400–2100.* Loads of wines and a few dishes to soak up the alcohol.

Het Molenpad Prinsengracht 653 (625 9680) *Open Sun–Thur 1200–0100; Fri, Sat 1200–0200.* A dimly lit cosy brown bar with soothing music and, in the summer, tables spilling outside to the canal. Located near lots of antique shops, it has a terrace overlooking the canal and a small art gallery for local artists.

Hof van Holland Rembrandtplein 5 (626 5649) *Opening times vary.* Football fans will enjoy the soccer theme.

In de Olofspoort Nieuwebrugsteeg 13 (624 3918) *Open Tues–Thur 1700–0100; Fri, Sat 1700–0200.* Good choice of liqueurs and *jenevers*.

In de Waag Nieuwmarkt (422 7772) *Open daily 1000–0100.* Candles light this pleasant café which is in an old weigh house.

In de Wildeman Kolksteeg 3 (638 2348) *Open Mon–Sat 1200–0100; Sun 1400–2100.* A *bierproeflokaal*, a beer-tasting house with a lovely old bar and more than 170 bottled beers and nearly 20 on tap. Also a big choice of schnapps here, as well as live traditional music at weekends. Unusually, there's also a non-smoking room.

In 't Aepjen (The Monkey) Zeedijk 1 (626 8401) *Open daily 1500–0100.* Zeedijk is the city's original dockside street and this bar, housed in one of Amsterdam's oldest buildings (built in the 16th century as a lodging house) and full of curios, helps capture the spirit of those long-ago days. The name of the bar originates from the time when sailors would pawn their exotic pets collected on their travels, to pay for their lodgings. On Saturday nights accordionist Herman de Neus plays traditional Dutch ditties and sea shanties, and it's very popular with the locals.

Kapitein Zeppo's Gebed Zonder End 5 (624 2057) *Open Sun–Thur 1100–0100; Fri, Sat 1100–0300.* A bar with an old feel, for a young crowd.

Katte in 't Wijngaert Lindengracht 160 (622 4554) *Open Sun–Thur 1000–0100; Fri, Sat 1000–0300.* Jordaan café.

Kingfisher Ferdinand Bolstraat 23 (671 2395) *Open Mon–Thur 1300–0100; Fri, Sat 1300–0300.* Pleasant brown café in the Pijp.

Land van Walem Keizersgracht 449 (625 3544) *Open daily*

1030–0100. A modern *eetcafé/*café bar with a canal-side terrace.

Last Waterhole Oudezijds Armsteeg 12 (624 4814) *Opening times vary*. Popular with backpackers, this bar has pool tables and live rock or blues on Friday and Saturday evenings.

Lokaal 't Loosje Nieuwmarkt 32–34 (627 2635) *Open Sun–Thur 1000–0100; Fri, Sat 1000–0200*. An ex-tram waiting room with attractive etched glass windows and tile tableaus on the walls which has turned into a well-established brown café that's ever popular with the locals.

L'Opera Rembrandtplein (627 5232) *Open Sun–Thur 1000–0100; Fri, Sat 1000–0200*. Grand café for tourists rather than locals with overpriced coffees to match.

Molly Malone's Oudezijds Kolk 9 (624 1150) *Open Sun–Thur 1100–0100; Fri, Sat 1100–0200*. Irish bar.

Morlang Keizersgracht 451 (625 2681) *Open Sun–Thur 1030–0100; Fri, Sat 1030–0200*. A bar in an old house with a pleasant terrace to enjoy a drink.

Mulligans Amstel 100 (622 1330) *Open Mon–Thur 1600–0100; Fri 1600–0300; Sat 1400–0300; Sun 1400–0100*. Popular Irish pub with live (FREE) music many evenings from around 2100.

O'Donnell's Ferdinand Bolstraat 5 (676 7786) *Open Sun–Thurs 1100–0100; Fri, Sat 1100–0300*. Irish pub in the Pijp with Guinness and Kilkenny beers, live Irish music and a large terrace.

Oininio Café Prins Hendrikkade 20–21 (553 9326) *Open daily 1100–0100*. A grand café opposite Centraal Station.

Oosterling Utrechsestraat 140 (623 4140) *Opening times vary.* 300-year-old brown café.

O'Reilly's Irish Pub Paleisstraat 103–105 (624 9498) *Open Sun– Thur 1100–0100; Fri, Sat 1100–0300.* Irish pub that is especially popular with the city's Irish community.

Ot Doktertje (Little Doctor) Rozenboomsteeg 4 (626 4427) *Open Tues–Sat 1600–0100.* A 200-year-old ex-surgery, this is Amsterdam's smallest brown café. It has lots of decoration.

Pilsner Club Begijnsteeg 4 (623 1777) *Opening times vary.* A small brown café that opened in 1893 and which has apparently changed little since then.

Proust Noordermarkt 4 (623 9145) *Opening times vary.* Modern café bar with live jazz/blues on Thursdays 2100, Sundays 1600.

Pygmalion Nieuwe Spiegelstraat (420 7022) *Open Sun–Thur 1100–0100; Fri, Sat 1100–0200.* Sit back with an excellent coffee to a background of 1940s big band jazz in a cosy café with yellow-painted plaster walls, and fake cracks painted on to give an aged look.

Rick's Café Oudezijds Voorburgwal (622 9658) *Open Sun–Thur 1100–0100; Fri, Sat 1100–0200.* Packed, wild and noisy bar.

Scheltema Neiuwezijds Voorburgwal 242 (623 2323) *Opening times vary.* A brown café traditionally popular with newspaper sleuths.

Slijterij Tapperij Oosterling Utrechtsestraat 140 (623 4140) *Open Mon–Sat 1300–0100, Sun 1300–2000.* Good *proeflokaal.*

Spanjer en Van Twist Leliegracht 60 (639 0109) *Opening times* *vary*. A modern *eetcafé* serving omlettes in earthenware pots, and sandwiches.

Thijssen Brouwersgracht 107 (623 8994) *Open Sun–Thur 0930–0100; Fri, Sat 0930–0300*. Popular bar in the Jordaan.

Three Sisters Rembrandtplein 17 (622 8109) *Open Sun–Thur 1100–0100; Fri, Sat 1100–0200*. A busy central pub with an elegant frontage and large terrace.

Turquoise Wolvenstraat 22 (624 2026) *Opening times vary*. Turkish *eetcafé* with inexpensive dishes.

Van Kerkwijk Nes 41 (620 3316) *Open Mon–Thur, Sun 1100–0100; Fri, Sat 1100–0300*. Specialises in wines.

Van Puffelen Prinsengracht 377 (624 6270) *Open Sun–Thur 1500–0100; Fri, Sat 1800–2300*. Live jazz on Sundays at this spacious brown café.

VOC Café Schreierstoren, Prins Hendrikkade 94 (428 8291) *Open Mon–Thur 1000–0100; Fri, Sat 1000–0300; Sun 1200–2000*. The Schreierstoren, or 'Weeping Tower' was Amsterdam's oldest defence tower and is now a pleasant bar with terraces with regular live accordion and similar music.

Walem Keizersgracht 449 (625 3544) *Open daily 1000–0100*. A modern, spacious bar with a summer garden and terrace overlooking the canal.

Welling Jan Willem Brouwerstraat 32 (662 0155) *Open Mon–Fri 1600–2400; Sat, Sun 1500–0100*. Good choice of beers at this bar in the museum quarter.

Wild Style Oudezijds Voorburgwal (625 9680) *Opening times vary*. A lively bar catering for a younger crowd.

Wijnand Fockinck Pijlsteeg 31 (639 2695) *Open daily 1500–2100.* A busy *proeflokaal* without seating near the Dam with a wide selection of spirits, schnapps and liqueurs with intriguing names like 'Parrot Soup'. In the summer you can lounge in the pretty garden courtyard, where tables sit among trees and fountains.

Chess

Max Euwe Centrum Max Euweplein 30A, off Leidseplein (625 7017, www.maxeuwe.nl) *Open Tues–Fri and first Sat of month 1030–1600.* Chess lovers will enjoy Amsterdam's homage to the Netherlands' only world chess champion, Max Euwe. You can play against chess computers or real people, and there is an international library and various artefacts relating to chess.

Schaakcafé 't Hok Lange Leidsedwarsstraat 134 (624 3133) Enthusiasts of the game hang out here.

Schaak en Go het Paard Haarlemmerdijk 147 (624 1171) *Open Tues–Sat 1030–1730.* A shop specialising in chess sets.

Children's Amsterdam

Amsterdam, being so compact, is ideal for children. With such a concentration of historic buildings, and regular church bell carillons, the city feels rather fairy tale-like, another plus for children. Amsterdam's children tend to be very relaxed and confident, maybe because of the easy-going nature of their parents. They are allowed in pubs, and the age of consent is 12.

If you do take children, just keep them away from the red light district and those cannabis dens, the coffee shops. With young children you do, of course, have to be more vigilant than normal since there is so much water around. There are also all the trams and bicycles to avoid as well as cars.

A few hotels have a policy not to admit children, so check beforehand. Many restaurants and cafés have high chairs and children's menus, but there are few nappy-changing facilities apart from at Centraal Station and the biggest stores. Opening times and admission prices for museums mentioned here can be found in the 'Museums and Collections' section of the book.

Ajax Museum Arena Boulevard 3, Zuid Oost (311 1469/428 4920) *Open daily 1000–1800 although can vary on match days. Adults f15/E6.75, under-12s f12.50/E5.65.* Great for young football fans, this museum at the home team's new stadium covers the long history of this famous club.

Amsterdamse Bos A huge wood planted in the 1930s where you can hire pedaloes and canoes. There are playgrounds, bike hire, a picnic area, riding stables, a buffalo and bison reserve and a goat farm. The Bosmuseum (Koenenkade 56, Amsterdamse Bos, tel. 676 2152) is a free museum explaining the formation of the Amsterdamse Bos. Children love the woodland grotto, which turns from night to day.

Animals see 'Animal Enclosures and City Farms', page 32.

Anne Frankhuis (Anne Frank's House) Prinsengracht 267 (556
7100, www.annefrank.nl) *Open Jan–Mar, Sept–Dec daily
0900–1900; Apr–Aug daily 0900–2100. Closed Dec 25, 1 Jan,
Yom Kippur. Admission: adults f12.50/E5.65, 10–17s f7.50/
E3.40.* Of course children can relate easily to Anne Frank's
House and the horror of the Nazi death camps as she was
just a small girl when she lived here. The realities of the
German Occupation are made vivid when they learn of
Anne's life of hiding in the attic, not going out, not seeing
friends and not having sweets. Go early or late to beat the
queues.

Aviodome (National Aviation Museum) Westelijke Randweg 201,
Schiphol Centre, Zuid (406 8000, www.aviodome.nl) *Open Apr–
Sept daily 1100–1700; Oct–Mar Tues–Fri 1100–1700; Sat, Sun
1200–1700. Adults f15/E6.75, children over 4 f12.50/E2.50.*
Children love the 25 historic aircraft here, and can climb
into cockpits and use the flight simulator.

Babysitting Many hotels can arrange this or try these
agencies: Oppascentrale De Peuterette, Hectorstraat 20
(679 6793) or OppasCentrale Kriterion, Roetersstraat 170h
(624 5848).

Beaches Zandvoort has a good 15-km/9-mile-long beach
and is just a short train ride away.

Boat Trips With canals and bridges making up so much of
Amsterdam, children love a boat ride. Many boats depart
from a variety of spots around Centraal Station and Damrak
every 15 minutes or so. You could also hire a canal bike.
See 'Boat Tours and Rentals', page 52.

Climbing Church Towers The Westerkerk (West Church),

Prinsengracht 279 Wester Markt (624 7766, tower 552 4169) has the highest tower in Amsterdam, while the Zuiderkerk, Zuiderkerkhof 72 (689 2565) also provides a bird's eye view of central Amsterdam.

Clothes Shops for Kids These are expensive, but fun for window-shopping: BamBam (Magna Plaza, Nieuwezijds Voorburgwal 182); Exota Kids (Nieuwe Leliestraat 32); and Storm (Magna Plaza, Nieuwezijds Voorburgwal 182, tel: 624 1074). Prenatal (Kalverstraat 40, 626 6392) has more down-to-earth prices; it's a sort of Dutch Mothercare.

Cycling There are are lots of outlets that hire out bikes and children's seats. See 'Cycling' page 85.

Electrische Museum Tramlijn Amsterdam (Electric Tram Museum) Haarlemmermeer Station, Amstelveenseweg 264, Amstelveen (673 7538/423 1100, www.trammuseum.demon.nl) *Open Apr–Oct Wed 1345–1515; Sun, public holidays 1100–1700. Adults ƒ6.60/E3, children ƒ3.30/E1.50.* Ride in an historic tram to the Amsterdamse Bos, a one-hour round trip.

Ferry Ride Young children love the FREE ferry ride behind Centraal Station (landing stage 7/8, de Ruijterkade; operates daily every 5–10 minutes or so) over the IJ, the oldest part of Amsterdam's port. Although this trip to north Amsterdam only lasts a few minutes, there are splendid views of the expanse of water. There's little of interest directly on the other side, but about three miles on there's good countryside.

Jaap Edenbaan Radioweg 64 (694 9894) Has indoor and outdoor ice-skating rinks.

KinderKookKafe Oudezijds Achterburgwal 193 (625 3257) *Times and costs vary, booking in advance essential.* This novel restaurant runs afternoon cookery courses for children (high teas are handled by the under-8s, dinner by 8–12-year-olds) and on Saturdays and Sundays the children run the whole show, cooking, serving and washing up. The simple meals are inexpensive and parents/guardians and friends can sit down for the meal. English-speaking children are well catered for.

Kindermuseum (Children's Museum) Linnaeusstraat 2 (568 8300, www.tropenmuseum.nl) *Open Mon, Wed–Fri 1000–1630; Tues 1000–2130; Sun 1200–1630. Adults f12.50/E5.65, children 6–17 f7.50/E3.50.* This is a museum specifically for 6–12-year-olds. As it is quite heavily Dutch in presentation it would appeal most to more independently minded children. You book a 90-minute session for the child, and the museum introduces children to different cultures using hands-on displays. It is attached to the Tropenmuseum (Tropical Museum).

Madame Tussauds Scenerama Dam 20 (622 9239, www. madame-tussauds.com) *Open daily 1000–1730. Adults f19.95/ E9.00.* Wax museum that's ever-popular with kids.

Nederlands Scheepvaartmuseum (Netherlands Maritime Museum) Kattenburgerplein 1 (523 2222, www.scheepvaart museum.nl) *Open Sept–June Tue–Sun 1100–1700; July/Aug daily 1100–1700. Adults f14.5/E6.50, concessions f8–f12.50, E3.60–E5.60.* Aspiring sailors will enjoy the comprehensive collection of naval memorabilia. There are model boats and a full-sized replica Dutch East India Company ship to explore.

newMetropolis Science and Technology Center Oosterdok 2 (531 3233, informationline 0900 919 1100, www.newmetropolis.nl/ www.newmet.nl) *Open Tues–Sun 1100–1700. Admission f18.75/E8.00.* Aimed at educating kids, this striking copper-green building which from the outside looks like a green boat coming out of the water, has many interactive exhibits, computer games and videos covering subjects such as transport, energy, communications, music and the brain. There are lots of films, workshops, demonstrations and exhibitions.

Pancake Bakery Prinsengracht 191 (625 1333) *Open daily 1200–2130.* This lovely, cosy, very child-friendly pancake house on a very pleasant stretch of the Prinsengracht claims to bake the best pancakes in town (from f9.50/E4.30) and it's easy to believe. There are over 70 varieties and kids can draw with crayons while they're waiting.

Puppet Theatre (627 9188) From May to October on Wednesday afternoons a theatre is held on Dam Square unless it is raining. Then, and from November to April on Sunday afternoons, the theatre is held under cover in St Pietespoortsteeg. Also there are shows put on at Amsterdam Marionettentheater, Nieuwe Jonkerstraat 8 (620 8027).

Rijksmuseum Stadhouderskade 42 (674 7047, www.rijks museum.nl) *Open daily 1100–1700. Adults f15/E6.75, under-18s FREE.* Although being dragged round the 200 or so rooms of this huge museum is the last thing the average child would relish, some exhibits would interest them. Rembrandt's *The Night Watch in the Gallery of Honour* on the first floor is impressive, not least because of its size. There are some beautiful 17th- and 18th-century dolls' houses, impeccably furnished with great attention to detail including monogrammed napkins, real marble floors and silk tapestries. Outside the museum there's often some sort of street entertainment, and a pleasant garden with statuary and fountains to rest in when the little ones get weary.

Swimming See page 166.

Toy Shops Adults, as well as UK children reared on Toys 'R' Us, will love the toy shops of Amsterdam which sell traditional wooden toys, puppets and dolls' houses. They include: **Bell Tree** Spiegelgracht 10 (625 8830); near the Rijksmuseum is **De Speelmuis** Elandsgracht 58 (638 5342) Miniature toys, dolls' houses, etc.; **De Zeiling** Ruysdaelstraat 21–23 (679 3817) Wooden toys and other traditional items; **Joe's Vliegerwinkel** Nieuwe Hoogstraat 19 (625 0139) Kites, boomerangs and yo-yos; **Kitch Kitchen Kids** Rozengracht 183 (622 8261) Stock includes lively Mexican toys; **Knuffels** Nieuwe Hoogstraat 11 (427 3862) Colourful mobiles, soft toys, etc.; **Mechanisch Speelgoed** Westerstraat 67 (638 1680) Traditional toys like wind-up toys and puppets; **Mr Kramer** Reestraat 18–20 (626 5274) Many antique dolls with cute doll hospital; **Pinkkio** Magna Plaza, Nieuwezijds Voorburgwal 182 (622 8914) Pinocchio dolls, rocking horses, wooden toys; **Schaal Treinen Huis** Bilderdijkstraat 94 (612 2670) Modelling kits, model trains and cars, dolls' houses and accessories.

Tram Tour Take the Circle Tram (number 20) which passes most of the museums, churches, bridges and canals. The ticket is available from the Tourist Information Board, GVB branches, some hotels and on the tram itself. A one-day pass costs adults f12/E5.40, children f7/E3.15.

Tropenmuseum (Tropical Museum) Linnaeusstraat 2 (568 8200, www.tropenmuseum.nl) *Open Mon, Wed–Fri 1000–1630; Tues 1000–2130; Sun 1200–1630. Adults f12.50/E5.65, children 6–17 f7.50/E3.40.* This has walk-in life-sized touch, smell and listen dioramas of life in the tropics and subtropics, which are inspiring for children. The café at the museum offers dishes from around the world, a further enjoyable educational activity. It is attached to the Kindermuseum (Children's Museum). See 'Kindermuseum' page 77.

Vondelpark *Open 24 hours a day.* This is a safe and friendly park right in the centre of the city with lakes, cafés, lawns, waterways and gardens. There is an animal enclosure, street entertainers and a good children's playground.

Winkel Noordermarkt 43 *Open Mon–Sat 0800–1700.* Kids will love the cakes and strudels at this popular tea room on the corner of Noordermarkt Square.

Cinema

In Amsterdam films in English are usually subtitled and are seldom dubbed, although children's films are more likely to be dubbed. 'AL' is short for *alle leeftijden*, meaning the film is suitable for all ages, and a film marked 12 or 16 indicates the minimum age allowed.

Cinecenter Lijnbaansgracht 236 (623 6615) An interesting, mixed programme avoiding the usual Hollywood fare.

Desmet Plantage Middenlaan 4a (627 3434) Ornate art deco cinema which was used by a Jewish cabaret company in World War II. It is now an art cinema.

De Uitkijk Prinsengracht 452 (623 7460) In a canal house, this is the city's oldest cinema, dating from 1913.

Goethe Institut Herengracht 470 (623 0421) The German cultural centre shows some films with English subtitles.

Kriterion Roetersstraat 170 (623 1709) Art and cult films.

Nederlands Filmmuseum Vondelpark 3 (589 1400, www.nfm.nl) *Admission f12.50/E5.65.* The Dutch equivalent of the UK's National Film Theatre shows several new and classic films a day. At the north-west entrance of Vondelpark, this restored mansion has an elegant pavilion facade and inside the interior of the Cinema Parisien, the city's first cinema, which was built in 1910 and saved from demolition in 1987. On Saturdays from late May/early June to late August, as part of the Vondelpark Openluchttheater (673 1499, www.openluchttheatter.nl) season, the Filmmuseum has FREE screenings on the terrace.

The Movies Haarlemmerdijk 161 (638 6016) A popular cinema retaining its 1920s interior.

Tuschinski Cinema Reguliersbreestraat 26–28 (0900 1458) You can still sip champagne by the glass during the intermission at this magnificent art deco ex–variety theatre from the '20s.

Coffeeshops (*Koffieshops*)

Confusingly, the emphasis here is on marijuana rather than coffee. In these shops the sale and smoking of it is tolerated. It's one major area (the other is the huge sex industry) where the city's famous liberalism lives on. The attitude to soft drugs like marijuana demonstrates typical Amsterdam tolerance. So that cannabis smokers are not driven underground, an official blind eye is turned to the use of the substance in these coffeeshops.

Remember though that, even though coffeeshops exist, drugs are not legal in the Netherlands. People found with hard drugs such as heroin and cocaine can expect the matter not to be treated lightly by the authorities.

On the subject of drugs, a number of so-called 'smart drug shops' have sprung up in Amsterdam in recent years. They sell natural hallucinogens like aphrodisiacs, herbal cigarettes, magic mushrooms, opium and marijuana seeds, with the approval of the Dutch Ministry of Health, which considers them safe when used sensibly, although other Ministries of Health may disagree. If you do choose to buy from these shops, be sure to ask what is considered a safe dosage and what exactly to expect. And don't expect British customs to greet you and your purchases with welcoming open arms.

Back to the coffeeshops, quality and price of the dope can vary greatly, but is usually very acceptable. See the menu in the shop for further details. Many of Amsterdam's 300 coffeeshops (look out for the palm leaves and red, gold and green Rastafarian colours as an indicator of many) are mangy tips, especially in the red light district, but in recent years a number of bright, airy and attractive ones have opened and are more appealing, even if you don't want a smoke. There are also some *hashcafés* which much resemble pubs.

By the way, although it is acceptable to smoke dope in coffeeshops, it is not done to do so in public – the locals strongly dislike seeing foreigners doing so. And don't buy drugs on the street: you are likely to be mugged or conned or will create problems for yourself with the police.

Warning: smoking too much dope can make you very, very boring.

Barney's Haarlemmerstraat 102 (625 9761) *Open daily 0700–2000.* Coffeeshop that has branched out into a variety of all-day breakfasts.

Bulldog Leidseplein 13–17 (627 1908) One of a chain of five in Amsterdam.

De Kuil Oudebrugsteeg 27 (623 4848) *Open Sun–Thur 1200– 2400; Fri 1200–0100; Sat 1200–0300. Metro Centraal Station.* A pleasant cross between brown café and coffeeshop.

De Rokerij Lange Leidsedwarsstraat 41 (622 9442); also at Singel 8 (422 6643). *Open Sun–Thur 1000–0100; Fri, Sat 1000–0300.* This is very popular in the evenings and has an African and Oriental theme.

Global Village Chill-Out Lounge Kerkstraat 51 (639 1154) *Opening times vary.* Comfy couches and laid-back tunes.

Greenhouse Oudezijds Voorburgwal 191 (627 1739); also Water-looplein 345 (622 5499) *Open Sun–Thur 0900–0100; Fri, Sat 0900–0300.* Knowledgeable, helpful staff and a good selection make this very popular.

Greenhouse Effect Warmoestraat 53–55 (623 7462) *Open Sun– Thur 0900–0100; Fri, Sat 0900–2000.* Another option for cannabis connoisseurs.

Gray Area Oude Leliestraat 2, Jordaan (420 4301) *Open Tues–Sun 1200–2000*. Friendly with good quality stock.

Homegrown Fantasy Nieuwezijds Vorrburgwal 87a (627 5683) *Open Sun–Thur 0900–2400; Fri, Sat 0900–0100*. This red light district coffeeshop has an extensive choice of weed and even eight types of Rizlas.

Kadinsky Rosemarijnsteeg 9 (624 7023) *Open daily 1000–0100*. Homely and welcoming with an extensive menu.

La Tertulia Prinsengracht 312 *Open Tues–Sat 1100–1900*. On a beautiful section of canal and if dope's not your thing it has lots of teas to sample.

Paradox 1e Bloemdwarsstraat 2 (623 5639) *Open daily 1000–2000*. A good food selection as well as the hash.

Pi Kunst and Koffie Tweede Laurierdwarsstraat 64 (622 5960) *Open Sun–Wed 1000–2000, Thur–Sat 1000–2100*. Coffee-shop on the canal with chess and backgammon sets.

Rookies Korte Leidsedwarsstraat 145 (622 9442) *Open daily 1000–2000*. Just off the Leidseplein, this friendly coffee shop has a pool table and tables outside.

Sensi Smile Coffee Shop Oude Doelenstraat 20 (623 5267) *Opening times vary*. A mellow hangout with trippy music and an upstairs room covered with Persian rugs and low tables.

Siberie Brouwersgracht 11 (623 5909) *Open daily 1100–2300*. Popular, not least because of its comedy, poetry and music events.

T-Boat Oudeschans, opposite no. 141 (423 3799) *Open Sun–*

Thur 1100–1800; *Fri, Sat* 1000–2400. Of course, someone had to put a coffeeshop on a boat and this is it.

Cycling

Newcomers to Amsterdam are usually surprised at the huge number of bikes in the city. There's well over half a million of them. The multi-storey bike park by Centraal Station is certainly a memorable sight. The popularity of cycling in Amsterdam is understandable: the city is not particularly car-friendly, parking is scarce and it is small enough to be easily navigable on two wheels. Bicycles are so popular that Amsterdammers reckon the canals are three metres deep, made up of one of water, one of mud and one of rusty old bikes.

Although there are bicycle lanes on most roads, if you're not used to the city there are the trams and tram lines to contend with, mad local cyclists and complicated traffic lights (which control the cars, trams and cycles). Bear in mind that cycling two abreast is illegal, reflector bands are required on both wheels, and the chance of having your bike stolen is comparatively high (around 200,000 are nicked each year), so use a sturdy lock.

Most bikes in the city were not built particularly for speed or traction. Few have lights or gears, many look cumbersome and uncared for – probably so that no one will be tempted to steal them. Beware that mopeds use cycle paths too and often don't keep to the speed limit.

Dutch cyclists are as likely to ride on the pavement as the

road, and you're likely to see parents carrying one child at the front and one at the back, lots of pillion passengers, and laid-back Amsterdammers on their bicycles eating, drinking, smoking, reading a map, clutching a pet animal or chatting away on a mobile phone, deftly dodging the trams and pedestrians as they do so.

Plenty of firms hire bikes, including the following. Hire charges typically start at around f10–15 (E4.50–6.75) for the first day. Many can supply free route maps and suggestions. Ensure the bike comes with a lock.

Drug addicts regularly offer stolen bikes at very low prices, but as it is a relatively widespread problem, if you are caught with a stolen bike the Amsterdam police treat the matter very seriously.

Finally, don't forget that beautiful countryside dotted with windmills is just 30 minutes out of the city by bike.

Amstel Rijwielshop Julianaplein 1 (692 3584) *Open Mon–Fri 0600–2400; Sat 0730–2400.*

Amstel Stalling Amstelstation (692 3584).

Bike City Bloemgracht 68 (626 3721) *Open daily, times vary but usually 0900–1800.*

Cycle Tours Keizersgracht 181 (627 4098).

Damstraat Rent-a-Bike Pieter Jacobsz Dwarsstraat 11 (625 5029).

Fietseria Amstelveenseweg 880–900 (644 5473) *Open Mon–Fri 1000–1800.*

Holland Rent-a-Bike Damrak 247 (622 3207) *Open Mon–Wed,*

Fri 0700–1900; Thur 0700–2100; Sat 0800–1800; Sun 0900–1800.

Koenders Take-A-Bike Centraal Station, Stationsplein 12 (624 8391) *Open daily 0800–2400.*

Macbike Mr Visserplein 2 (620 0985) *Open daily 1000–1800.*

Macbike Too Marnixstraat 220 (626 6964) *Open daily 0900– 1800.*

Rent-A-Bike Damstraat 22 (625 5029) *Open daily 0900–1800.*

Sint Nicolaas Rent-a-Bike Sint Nicolaasstraat 16 (623 9715).

Take-a-bike rentservice Zijwind, Van Ostadestraat 108–110 (673 7026) *Open Tues–Fri 0900–1800; Sat 0900–1800.*

Yellow Bike Nieuweezijds Kolk 29 (620 6940).

Diamonds

Since the diamond trade was introduced to Amsterdam by Sephardic Jews in the 16th century, the city has been a centre of diamond cutting. During World War II more than 2,000 Jewish diamond polishers from Amsterdam disappeared into concentration camps in Germany and Poland.

Some of the world's most famous diamonds have been cut and polished in Amsterdam, including the Cullinan diamond, the largest ever found, as well as the smallest. The *Koh-i-Noor* (Mountain of Light), which is now in the collection of British crown jewels, was cut here.

Today, it is still possible to see diamond cutters at work. Five diamond firms offer FREE guided tours of their works, where you can find out how a diamond is chosen, sawn and valued and get to see the diamonds being polished and set in gold. Usually there's a mini-museum of antique equipment and other related items.

Unless you're in a big group, look very rich or unhealthily interested in gems, you'll probably be whisked around in a few minutes. But all these firms also offer FREE tea, coffee and soft drinks afterwards, so it's worth enduring five minutes of their banter to obtain a free drink in their centrally located, pleasant cafés rather than buying an overpriced coffee in a grotty, crowded tourist café nearby.

Amsterdam Diamond Center Rokin 1–5 (624 5787) *Open daily 1000–1800, but occasionally varies.*

Coster Diamonds Paulus Potterstraat 2–6 (305 5555) *Open daily 0900–1700.*

Gassan Diamonds Nieuwe Uilenburgerstraat 173–175 (622 5333) *Open daily 0900–1700.* When I visited, I was treated to an engaging commentary and all questions were answered comprehensively. It was enthralling when £500,000 of diamonds were spilled out in front of me. Sometimes Gassan even offers to polish visitors' jewellery or provide a complimentary chauffeur service.

Stoeltie Diamonds Wagenstraat 13–17 (623 7601) *Open daily 0900–1700.*

Van Moppes and Zoon Diamonds Albert Cuypstraat 2–6 (676 7601) *Open daily 0845–1745.*

Gay Amsterdam

Amsterdam is often regarded as the gay and lesbian capital of Europe and is well known to have much to offer, especially for gay men. There are over 100 bars, nightclubs, hotels, shops and discos specifically geared to a gay crowd, especially around Reguliersdwarsstrat, Amstel and Rembrandtplein, Warmoesstraat and Kerkstraat.

Regulierstraat, Amstel and Rembrandtplein have many gay bars, clubs, cafés and restaurants, while Warmoesstraat, in the red light district, is the place for clubs featuring leather, rubber, hard-core porn and all the rest.

Gay venues often have FREE magazines, leaflets and maps about the current gay events and places to go in Amsterdam.

The Gay and Lesbian Switchboard (623 6565) Advises on current clubs and other developments.

COC Rozenstraat 14 (623 4079/626 3087) The city's gay cultural and social centre. It has a café and organises weekly lesbian and gay discos.

Homomonument In the shadow of the Westerkerk at Westermarkt is a monument comprised of three triangles of pink granite which form a larger triangle. It is the world's first memorial to gays and lesbians persecuted by the Nazis.

The Pink Point of Presence *June–Aug, daily, 1200–1800.* A kiosk adjacent to the Homomonument called the Pink Point of Presence (playing on the title of the tourist information organisation VVV) stocks information including FREE magazines and maps, all geared to gay visitors.

Zandvoort On the coast, a 30-minute train ride from Centraal Station, Zandvoort is considered to be 'Amsterdam's beach' due to its popularity with the city. It has a gay beach complete with two gay bars, Eldorado and Sans Tout.

GAY ANNUAL EVENTS

Koninginnedag (Queen's Day) *30 April* Amsterdam is filled with thousands of revellers on this day, and the Homomonument at Westermarkt is the centre of lesbian and gay celebrations known as the *Roze Wester* (Pink Wester) featuring live music and street dancing.

Homosexual Remembrance Day Homomonument, Westermarkt *4 May*. Dutch gay organisation COC has its own ceremony to remember the homosexuals who died during World War II.

EuroPerve *Last Saturday in May (620 5603)*. This event, serving the more sexually adventurous, consists of music, dancing, performances and more, with the dress code leather, latex and the like.

AIDS Memorial Day Beurs van Berlage. *Last Saturday in May*. After a ceremony where candles are lit, participants walk to Dam and release white balloons.

Amsterdam Gay Pride Weekend *First weekend of August*. The highlight is the canal parade, a magnificent floating display, as well as partying, sporting and cultural events and street performances around the city.

Amsterdam Leather Pride *1–2 weeks in late October*. Various organised parties and events.

World AIDS Day *1 December*. Various events around the city.

GAY CINEMA

Desmet Plantage Middenlaan 4a (627 3434) This ornate art deco cinema which is now an art cinema often shows gay films.

GAY NIGHTCLUBS

Argos Warmoesstraat 95 (622 6595) For men.

Exit Reguliersdwarsstraat 42 (625 8788) Spacious nightclub.

iT, Amstelstraat 24 (625 0111) Saturday is gays only at this flamboyant club.

Monopole Amstel 60 (624 6451) Loud disco at this gay brown café.

You II Amstel 178 (421 0900) Women-only night on Thursdays.

GAY RESTAURANTS, BARS AND CAFÉS

April Reguliersdwarsstraat 37 (625 9572) *Opening times vary*. Gay bar.

Cosmo Bar Kerkstraat 42 (624 8074) *Open daily 1400–0300*. Bar that stays open late.

De Spijker Kerkstraat 4 (620 5919) *Open daily 1000–1900*. Leather and moustaches is the dress code here.

Downtown Reguliersdwarsstraat 31 (622 9958) *Open daily 1000–1900*. Daytime *eetcafé*.

Getto Warmoestraat 51 (421 5151) *Open Thur–Sun 1700–0100*. American and British food in a campy joint popular both with gay men and lesbians. Womens, bingo, karaoke nights.

Havana Reguliersdwarsstraat 17 (620 6788) *Open Mon–Thur 1600–0100; Fri, Sat 1600–0200, Sun 1400–0100*. Lively bar.

Hemelse Modder Oude Wall 9 (624 3203) *Open Tues–Sun 1800–2400*. Romantic restaurant.

Huyschkaemer Utrechtsestraat 137 (627 0575) *Open Sun–Thur 1600–0100; Fri, Sat 1600–0300*. Restaurant popular with both gays and lesbians.

La Strada Nieuwezijds Voorburgwal 93 *Opening times vary*. Lesbian brown café hangout.

Lellebel Utrechtsestraat 4 (427 5139) *Opening times vary*. Transvestite performances Fri–Sun evenings.

Le Monde Rembrandtplein 6 (626 9922) *Open Sun–Thur 0900–0100; Fri, Sat 0900–0200*. A good *eetcafé* with terrace.

Montmartre Halve Maansteeg 10 (620 7622) *Open Sun–Thur 1700–0100; Fri, Sat 1700–0300*. Bar with singing contests.

Other Side Reguliersdwarsstraat 06 (421 1014) *Open daily 1100–0100*. Gay coffeeshop.

Queen's Head Zeedijk 20 (420 2475) *Open daily 2300–0400*. Café presided over by popular drag queen.

Saarein II Elandsstraat 119 (623 4901) *Opening times vary*. A beautiful 17th-century café especially popular with lesbians.

Soho Reguliersdwarsstraat 36 (626 1573) *Open Mon—Sat 2000—0400, Sun 1600—0300*. British-style pub.

Spanjer en van Twist Leliegracht 60 (639 0109) *Openening times vary*. Sandwiches and snacks at lunchtime, with romantic candle-lit dinners.

Vandenburg Lindengracht 95 (622 2716) *Open daily 1700—0100*. *Eetcafé* particularly popular with lesbians.

Vivelavie Amstelstraat 7 (624 0114) *Open daily 1500—0100*. Lively lesbian joint.

Web Sint Jacobsstraat 6 (623 6758) *Open Sun—Thur 1400—0100; Fri, Sat 1400—0230*. Men-only leather bar.

GAY SHOPS

Intermale Spuistraat 251 (625 0009) Gay magazines, books and videos.

Vrolijk Paliesstraat 135 (623 5142) Gay and lesbian magazines.

Vrouwen in Druk Westermarkt 5 (624 5003) Women's books.

Xanippe Unlimited Prinsengracht 290 (623 5854) Bookshop with good feminist and lesbian sections.

Gyms and Fitness Centres

Barry's Fitness Centre Lijnbaansgracht 350 (626 1036) *Admission prices and opening times vary*. Work those muscles to the disco beat.

Garden Gym Jodenbreestraat 158 (626 8772) *Open Mon, Wed, Fri, 0900–2300; Tues, Thur 1200–2300; Sat, Sun 1100–1830. Admission price varies.* Geared to gentler keep-fit regimes, for example low-impact aerobics.

Ice-skating

In winter, if the temperature drops sufficiently to freeze over the canals, Amsterdam is one big ice-skating rink. Of course this can be dangerous, so only skate where you see lots of other people doing so. Beware of skating under bridges and at the edges of canals – these areas do not always freeze as well.

Jaap Edenbaan Radioweg 64 (694 9894) This rink has indoor and outdoor ice-skating rinks. It is in the eastern district of Watergraafsmeer.

Lectures, Talks and Cultural Events

British Council Keizersgracht 269 (550 6060) Occasional events.

De Balie Kleine Gartmanplantsoen 10, Leidseplein (553 5151, www.balie.nl) *Open Sun–Thur 1000–0100; Fri, Sat 1000–0200.* Dutch cultural centre with a café, theatre and regular debates and seminars.

Goethe Institut Herengracht 470 (623 0421) German cultural centre with talks, discussions, exhibitions and films.

Italian Cultural Institute Keizersgracht 564 (626 5314) Occasional events.

John Adams Institute Herenmarkt 97 (624 7280) There are regular talks and lectures, often with internationally famous participants.

Vlaams Cultureel Centrum de Brakke Grond Nes 45 (622 9014) Flemish cultural centre with regular events.

The Life of a Ligger: There Is Such a Thing as a Free Lunch

If you have the ruthlessness, ingenuity, confidence, cheeky personality and possibly, sometimes, the stupidity required, you can turn the art of obtaining something for nothing, or getting in where you're not invited into something approaching a full-time occupation. This is never more valuable a skill than when you are travelling – especially when you are on a strict budget. Travel, especially in Europe, is seldom cheap.

This behaviour, known as 'ligging', 'blagging', or 'freeloading', is an especially popular pastime with many members of the media industry, who are almost required to master the art as part of their basic training.

And there's no end to it. With persistence, if you're able to pass yourself off as a half-competent hack travel writer, there are enough newspapers, magazines, airlines, ferry companies, car hire firms, tour operators and tourist offices out there to sponsor your trips to Amsterdam and elsewhere whether your piece actually appears in a publication or not.

But you need to be impudent enough to do it. If you possess this quality, one opportunity leads to another. You could, say, drop in on a freebie function such as the preview of a city centre art exhibition by entering at the same time as a group of others that you had seen who were about to walk in, or when the signing-in book was unattended.

Over the food and wine most generously provided by your host, you could see whether there are any parties happening later that evening. Obviously, attending one would mean that you won't be able to slip anonymously into a press screening of that big film you've been anxiously awaiting, that's showing in an hour in a neighbouring preview theatre.

The best way to deal with the PR people at the door of a promotional party, who are there to weed out hangers-on like you, is to make one of them think they've met you before. Public relations is all about meeting people all of the time, and they probably wouldn't know you from Adam even if they *had* once met you. So it's best to start the conversation by asking 'How are you? You've lost some weight/changed your hair. I suppose it's been a while.' Unless the PR person is absolutely *sure* you're an impostor, she's hardly going to risk causing a scene by ejecting you at such an important occasion.

Some other tips: if you want to avoid buying a round of drinks in a bar, drop down to tie a shoelace as the group approaches the bar, catching up with everyone when the round is bought.

A couple of waiters working in hotels recently confided to

me that they never bother to check whether names of hotel guests and their room numbers tally — indeed often they just request the room number from guests. The less moral would think it a pity not to use the opportunity such lack of diligence presents. To use bar and restaurant areas of larger hotels — small establishments may know patrons by sight — glimpse at the front desk as you enter to note how rooms are numbered: two digits or three for example. Such knowledge should suffice for provision of various hotel services, although it would be prudent to do some regular training of the 100-metre sprint prior to doing this.

It's best to visit restaurants in groups of at least 11 if the service charge is 10 per cent and groups of 13 if the service charge is 12.5 per cent. Get the group to agree beforehand to split the bill equally, saying that dissecting it with a calculator after the meal is tacky. When the bill comes, stress to the other members of the party how important it is to add 10 or 12.5 per cent to the total. This takes care of your share of the costs. It's a bit rotten to deprive the waiter or waitress of a tip, but at least you get a good meal for nothing.

Ligging opportunities are all around. If a crowd is walking into a house, a good ligger will always join them. There are endless excuses were he or she to be caught out. I mean, can you read half the house numbers clearly in a darkened street? It's best to go in brandishing a bottle of wine, which you can instantly return to the car on the pretext of having left your lights on by mistake.

Ligging is only at the expense of your conscience and

perception of morality. And at least if you go too far, accommodation will be free too − a spell in prison.

Markets

Albert Cuypmarkt Albert Cuypstraat *Open Mon−Sat 0930−1700*. Amsterdam's largest and busiest general market with food from all over the world, clothes, household items and more.

Amstelveld Flower Market Amstelveld *Open Mon 0900−1800*.

Antiekmearkt Nieuwmarkt (Nieuwmarkt Antiques Market) Nieuwmarkt *Open April–Sept Sun 0900−1700*.

Bird Market Noordermarkt, Noorderkerstraat *Open Sat 0800−1200*. The remains of the old livestock market, with caged birds, rabbits, guinea pigs etc.

Bloemenmarkt (Flower Market) Singel, between Muntplein and Koningsplein *Open Mon−Sat 0930−1700*. The world's only floating flower market, with a huge selection of plants, herbs and bulbs.

Boekenmarkt (Book Market) Spui *Open Fri 1000−1800*. Popular book market.

Boerenmarkt Around Noorderkerkstraat and Westerstraat *Open Sat 0900−1530*. FREE food and drink-tasting available at this popular organic food market that sells gifts and suchlike as well as organic food and drink.

Dappermarkt Dapperstraat, Oost *Open Mon−Sat 0900−1600*. A smaller general market favoured by locals.

Laspjesmarkt Westerstraat *Open Mon 0900–1300*. Fabric market.

Lindengracht General Market Lindengracht *Open Sat 0900–1700*.

Looier Markt Elandsgracht 109, Jordaan *Open Sat–Wed 1100–1700, Thur 1100–2100*. Antiques and collectables, with a number of individual stores each with a speciality.

Mosveldmarkt Mosveld, northern Amsterdam *Open Wed, Fri, Sat 1100–1700*. Non-touristy general market.

Noordermarkt Noorderkerstraat, Jordaan *Open Mon 0800–1400*. Adjacent to the Westermarkt, here you will find loads of antiques, clothes, jewellery etc.

Oudemanhuis Book Market Oudemanhuispoort *Open Mon–Fri 1100–1530*. A long-established book market in an 18th-century alley. Book lovers may also want to check out Spui Square on Fridays, where there is a small market.

Postzegelmarkt Nieuwezijds Voorburgwal, opposite 276, the Nova Hotel *Open Wed, Sat 1230–1600*. Coins, stamps, medals and the like.

Rommelmarkt Looiersgracht 38 *Open daily 1100–1700*. General bric-a-brac.

Spui Arts and Crafts Market Spui *Open Mar–Nov Sun 1030–1730*.

Thorbeckeplein Arts and Crafts Market Thorbeckeplein *Open Mar–Oct Sun 1100–1700*.

Veilinghuis Bezuyen Looiersgracht 38 *Open Sat–Thur 1100–*

1700. Jumble, from antiques to old clothes, books, CDs, furniture etc.

Waterlooplein Market Waterlooplein *Open Mon–Sat 0900–1700*. Touristy fleamarket with books, records, cheap and second-hand clothes, bric-a-brac etc, with lots of tat and a few treasures.

Westermarkt Westerstraat *Open Mon 0900–1230*. A general market run in conjunction with the Noordermarkt.

Moped Hire

Moped Rental Service Amsterdam Marnixstraat 208–210 (422 0266) *Open daily summer 0900–2000, winter 1200–1700*. You can hire a moped from f12.50/E5.65 for the first hour and it becomes cheaper for subsequent hours. No driver's licence or crash helmet are required surprisingly.

Museums and Collections

The Netherlands contains more museums per square metre than any other country and Amsterdam boasts around 50. Amsterdam has museums devoted to a wide range of subjects – including trams, erotica, tattoos, pianolas and cats. Around Museumplein, all just footsteps away from each other, stand the 'big three', the Rijksmuseum, the Van Gogh Museum and the Stedelijk Museum of Modern Art.

Admission is FREE unless otherwise stated.

Ajax Museum Amsterdam Arena, Arena Boulevard 3, Zuid Oost
(311 1469) *Open daily 1000–1800 although can vary on match
days. Adults f15/E6.75, under-12s f12.50/E5.65.* For football
fans, this south-of-the-centre museum located at the home
team's new stadium covers the long history of this famous
club, referred to by Amsterdammers as 'Sons of the Gods'.
As well as numerous historic and recent memorabilia and
exhibits, cups and trophies, there is a short film featuring
great goal scoring.

Allard Pierson Museum Oude Turfmarkt 127 (525 2556) *Open
Tues–Fri 1100–1700; Sat, Sun 1300–1700. Admission prices
vary.* Archaeological exhibits from Greece, Italy, Egypt and
the Near East including a collection of mummies.

**Amsterdams Historisch Museum (Amsterdam Historical
Museum)** Kalverstraat 92 (523 1822, www.ahm.nl) *Open Mon–
Fri 1100–1700; Sat, Sun 1100–1700. Adults f12/E5.40, concessions f6–9/E2.70–4.05.* This surprisingly interesting
museum covers the development of Amsterdam from the
13th century onwards, from a small fishing village to major
world capital. There are multimedia displays, archaeological exhibits, various models and many maps and pictures.
At the entrance is a FREE exhibition: the Schuttersgallerij
(Civil Guards Gallery). This a public thoroughfare with
several huge 16th- and 17th-century group portraits of rich
burghers on display. And the museum's café (which serves
delicious pancakes) houses a 17th-century wooden statue
of Goliath, over five metres high.

Anne Frankhuis (Anne Frank's House) Prinsengracht 267 (556
7100, www.annefrank.nl) *Open Sept–Mar daily 0900–1900;
Apr–Aug daily 0900–2100. Closed Dec 25, 1 Jan, Yom Kippur.*

Adults f12.50/E5.65, 10–17s f7.50/E3.40 FREE under-10s.
Go early or late to beat the queues at this very sad spot.
In this cramped 17th-century canal-side house the young
Jewish diarist and her family hid from the Germans for
more than two years during the occupation in World War
II. Anne, her sister and mother were then dragged off to
die in concentration camps. The house has been renovated,
but only to make it safe and the original wallpaper with
the pictures of film stars Anne stuck to the walls remains.
You see the false bookcase she and her family hid behind,
but there is no furniture as it was destroyed when the
residents were rounded up, and the Trustees of the house
wanted nothing added to the house which was not in place
when the Nazis knocked on the door. There is the bare
sink in the kitchen where the meagre meals were cooked,
and the exhibition includes displays concerning anti-Semi-
tism and neo-Fascism today as well as pictures and a video
showing the Frank family before they were taken to the
death camps. The house has recently been extended to
include father Otto Frank's jam factory.

Aviodome (National Aviation Museum) Westelijke Randweg 201,
Schiphol Centre, Zuid (406 8000, www.aviodome.nl) *Open Apr–
Sept daily 1100–1700; Oct–Mar Tues–Fri 1100–1700; Sat, Sun
1200–1700. Adults f15/E6.75, children over 4 f12.50/E5.65.*
There are 25 historic aircraft at this museum at Schipol
Airport, and exhibits cover the Wright Brothers' plane
used for the first motorised flight in 1903, a World War I
triplane, a 1911 Fokker, Spitfire, Dakota, as well as a look
at space travel. There's also a flight simulator.

Bedrijfsmuseum ENW Amsterdam Spaklerweg 20, Zuid (597

3107) Open by appointment. A small industrial museum focusing on gas and electricity.

Beurs van Berlage Museum (Stock Exchange Museum) Damrak 277; entrance at Beursplein 1 (530 4141) *Open (museum) Tues–Sun 1000–1600. Adult ƒ7/E3.15, child 12–16 ƒ4/E1.80, under-12s FREE.* Amsterdam's stock exchange, built 1897, is an architectural monument with an exhibition centre and museum on the history of the exchange. There are also two concert halls, a café, restaurant and an adjoining open-air tower that can be climbed.

Bijbels Museum (Bible Museum)) Herengracht 366–368 (624 2436) *Open Mon–Sat 1100–1700; Sun, bank holidays 1300–1700. Adults ƒ8/E3.60, 6–17s ƒ5.50/E2.50.* An impressive collection of bibles including the Delft bible printed in 1477, and archaeological displays illustrating life in biblical times including archaeological discoveries from Egypt and the Middle East. There are impressive 18th-century ceiling paintings by Jacob de Wit.

Bilderdijk Collection De Belelaan 1105, Zuid (444 5184) *Open by appointment.* A small collection concerned with Dutch 18th-century writer Willem Bilderdijk.

Bosmuseum Koenenkade 56, Amsterdamse Bos (676 2152) *Open daily 1100–1700.* The museum explains the formation of the Amsterdamse Bos, the vast forest built in the 1930s in which it is located. Children love the woodland grotto, which turns from night to day.

CoBrA Museum of Modern Art Sandbergplein 1, Amstelveen (547 5050) *Open Tues–Sun 1100–1700. Adults ƒ7.50/E3.40, concessions ƒ3.50–ƒ5/E1.60–2.25.* The name derives from the cities where the artists of the influential CoBRA art movement worked in the 1940s – Copenhagen, Brussels and Amsterdam.

Electrische Museum Tramlijn Amsterdam (Electric Tram Museum) Haarlemmermeer Station, Amstelveenseweg 264, Amstelveen (673 7538, www.trammuseum.demon.nl) *Open Apr–Oct Wed 1345–1515; Sun, public holidays 1100–1700. Adults f6.60/ E3, children f3.30/E1.50.* Collection of trams from Vienna, Amsterdam, the Hague, Rotterdam, Groningen, Utrecht and Prague built between 1910 and 1950, housed in a railway station dating from 1915. The museum also features an hour-long tram ride departing from Haarlemmermeer Station to the Amsterdamse Bos and Amstelveen.

Erotic Museum Oudezijds Achterburgwal 54 (624 7303) *Open Mon, Thur, Sun 1100–0100; Fri, Sat 1100–0200. Admission f5/E2.25.* Although containing some erotic sketches by John Lennon, this establishment stretches the term 'museum', with its collection of sex toys and artworks from around the world. It's about as erotic as a Wolverhampton bus shelter during a rain storm.

Geels and Co Koffie en Theemuseum (Geels and Co Coffee and Tea Museum) Warmesstraat 67 (624 0683) *Open: museum Sat 1200–1800; shop Mon–Sat 0930–1800.* This very well-stocked tea and coffee shop contains a small museum of brewing equipment, but be warned, we're not talking the British Museum here.

Hash Marijuana Hemp Museum Oudezijds Achterburgwal 148 (623 5961) *Open daily 1100–2200. Admission f8/E3.60.* Dedicated to all things hemp, with photos, memorabilia, pipes and press articles about the health and legal issues surrounding soft drugs. There is a room at the back where plants are growing, and a bookshop.

Heineken Browerij Museum (Heineken Brewery Museum) Stadhouderskade 78 (523 9239, information line 523 9666, www.heineken.nl) *Tours 16 Sept–May Mon–Fri 0930, 1100; June 1–Sept 15 Mon–Fri 0930, 1100, 1300, 1430. Charity donation: f2/E1. Over-18s only.* Heineken, the Dutch national beer, is the world's second largest brewing empire. This brewery, which operated from 1932 to 1988, is now a museum. The tour ends with a surprisingly generous beer-tasting. If it's your birthday and you can prove it, you get a free Delft blue beer mug.

Het Kattenkabinet (Cat Cabinet) Herengracht 497 (626 5378, www.kattenkabinet.nl) *Open Mon–Fri 1000–1400; Sat, Sun 1300–1700. Adults f10/E4.50, concessions f5/E2.25.* Everything from ancient Egyptian and Japanese netsuke, Picasso's *Le Chat*, paintings, posters, statuettes and a mannequin from the musical *Cats*. Even if you're not particularly interested in felines, the Kattenkabinet is one of Amsterdam's finest 17th-century canal side houses. If cats are your thing, also call in at de Poezenboot (the Cat Boat) opposite 20/40 Singel (see entry page 162).

Historisch Documentatiecentrum van de Vrije Universiteit De Boelelaan 1105, Zuid (444 7777) *Open Mon–Fri 0900–1645.* A historical research centre for the Dutch Protestant University.

Hollandse Schouwburg (Holland Theatre) Plantage Middenlaan 24 (626 9945) *Open daily 1100–1600, closed Yom Kippur.* Formerly a theatre that in 1942 became an assembly point for 60,000–80,000 Dutch Jews destined for the concentration camps. It is now a memorial to them. There are photos, film footage and other chilling memorabilia. A candle burns in a small chapel containing a wall with 6,700 surnames of the war victims, as a tribute to the 104,000 Dutch Jews who were killed in World War II.

Joods Historisch Museum (Jewish Historical Museum) Jonas Daniel Meijerplein 2–4 (626 9945, www.jhm.nl) *Open daily 1100–1700. Admission f8/E3.60, concessions f2–4/E1–1.80.* Four beautifully restored Ashkenazic synagogues built between 1671 and 1752 in the Jewish quarter make up this museum which houses religious exhibits covering the history of Judaism in the Netherlands.

Kantenhuis Kalverstraat 124 (624 8618) *Open Mon 1145–1800; Tues, Wed, Fri, Sat 0915–1800; Thur 0915–2100.* Fan collection.

Kindermuseum (Children's Museum) Linnaeusstraat 2 (568 8300, www.tropenmuseum.nl) *Open Mon, Wed–Fri 1000–1630; Tues 1000–2130; Sun 1200–1630. Adults f12.50/E5.65, children 6–17 f7.50/E3.50.* This is a museum specifically for 6–12-year-olds. As it is quite heavily Dutch in presentation it would appeal most to more independently minded children. You book a 90-minute session for the child, and the museum introduces children to different cultures using hands-on displays. It is attached to the Tropenmuseum (Tropical Museum).

Multatuli Museum Korsjespoortsteeg 20, Grachtengordel West (638 1938) *Open Tues 1100–1700; Sat, Sun 1200–1700.* Exhibits in the home of 19th-century Dutch writer Eduard Douwes-Dekker, who used the pseudonym Multatuli, which in Latin means 'I have suffered greatly'.

Museum Amstelkring Oudezijds Voorburgwal 40 (624 6604) *Open Mon–Sat 1100–1700; Sun 1300–1700. Adults f10/E4.50, concessions f6/E2.70.* Comparatively few visitors venture here, to this 17-century merchant's house, despite it containing the city's only remaining attic church, which was built in 1663. There are rooms furnished in the 17th-century style.

Museum Het Rembrandthuis (The Rembrandt House Museum) Jodenbreestraat 4–6 (520 0400, www.rembrandthuis.nl) *Open Mon–Sat 1100–1700; Sun 1300–1700. Adults f12.50/E5.65, concessions f2.50–10/E1.15–4.50.* Visit Rembrandt's home which has been recently restored to how it would have looked when he lived and worked there from 1639 until 1658. It houses a comprehensive collection of 250 etchings out of the 280 known to have been done by him, and temporary exhibitions. His son Titus was born in this house and his wife Saskia died here. There are drawings and paintings by his pupils and his teacher (Pieter Lastman). About the only thing missing are paintings by the man – most are in the US or at The Hermitage in St Petersburg.

Museum Vrolik AMC Medical Faculty, Meibergdreef 15, Zuidoost (566 9111) *Open Mon–Fri 1400–1700 and by appointment.* Specimens from the 18th and 19th centuries of human embryos and anatomy including congenital abnormalities, as well as tattooed skin samples.

Museum Willet-Holthuysen Herengracht 605 (523 1870) *Open daily 1100–1700. Adults f8/E3.60, 6–16s f4/E1.80.* This merchant's mansion built in 1687 which rather resembles a French chateau, is richly furnished in the neo-Louis XVI style and there's lots of silver, glassware, porcelain and pictures as well as an 18th-century formal French garden

---

with a sundial. You can see it for FREE if you peep through the fence at Amstelstraat.

Nationaal Brilmuseum Gasthuismolensteeg 7 (421 2414) *Open Wed–Fri 1200–1730; Sat 1200–1700. Admission f10/E4.50.* Both an opticians' museum and shop specialising in glasses both antique, old and new, with an exhibition on art, culture and 700 years of the spectacle.

Nederlands Scheepvaartmuseum (Netherlands Maritime Museum) Kattenburgerplein 1 (523 2222, www.scheepvaart museum.nl) *Open Sept–June Tue–Sun 1100–1700; July/Aug daily 1100–1700. Adults f14.5/E6.50, concessions f8–f12.50/ E3.60–E5.60.* One of Amsterdam's very best museums. In the heart of the naval district, a museum containing one of the world's most comprehensive collections of maritime memorabilia including 500 model boats, loads of maps and pictures and a full-sized replica Dutch East India Company ship to explore. It covers subjects that include the history of Dutch seafaring, whaling and naval warfare.

newMetropolis Science and Technology Center Oosterdok 2 (531 3233, informationline 0900 919 1100, www.newmet.nl) *Open Tues–Sun 1100–1700. Admission f18.75/E8.00.* Aimed at educating kids, this striking copper-green building which from the outside looks like a green boat coming out of the water, has many interactive exhibits, computer games and videos covering subjects such as transport, energy, communications, music and the brain. There are lots of films, workshops, demonstrations and exhibitions. If you get bored of making electricity or looking down microscopes, you can admire the great views from the rooftop plaza.

Open Haven Museum KNSM Laan 311 (418 5522) *Open Mon–Fri 1100–1700. Small admission charge for some exhibitions, otherwise FREE.* Changing exhibition of paintings, photos and objects relating to the history of the harbour, with bigger exhibitions sometimes in the grand hall upstairs.

Pianola Museum Westerstraat 106 (627 9624) *Open Sun 1300–1700; also opening can be arranged Mon–Fri for groups. Adults f8/E3.60, children f5/E2.25.* Exhibits relating to the pianola and mechanical musical machines.

Pijpenkabinet Prinsengracht 488 (421 1779, www.pijpen kabinet.nl) *Open Wed–Sat 1200–1800.* Collection of pipes and associated exhibits above a tobacco shop.

Rijksmuseum Stadhouderskade 42 (674 7047, www.rijks museum.nl) *Open daily 1100–1700. Adults f15/E6.75, under-18s FREE.* This 200-roomed national museum, a Dutch-style V&A, is the city's most popular sight, attracting more than 1.2 million visitors each year. A neoclassical, Dutch Renaissance building designed by Dutch architect P. J. H. Cuypers, it has a huge range of art treasures, from the masters of the Dutch Golden Age to the vast collection of sculpture and decorative arts. There is 17th-century furniture, intricate porcelain and silver, and a wealth of Dutch paintings dating from the 15th–19th century. Many visitors go straight to the 'Gallery of Honour' on the first floor, which is dominated by Rembrandt's *The Night Watch*. Nearby is another of his masterpieces, *The Syndics of the Drapers' Guild*. There's also Vermeer's *The Kitchen Maid* and *The Little Street*. Jan Steen, Frans Hals and Ferdinand Bol are also well represented. There are some beautiful 17th-and 18th-century dolls' houses, an engraved glass collection, a textile and costume collection and a fine collection of Asiatic art. Interiors from 18th-century Amsterdam have been reconstructed using original materials including panelling, carpets, curtains, wall coverings, chandeliers and furniture. The National Print Room contains about one million artworks including watercolours, woodcuts, photographs, engravings and etchings and has changing displays of a selection of these. There's a FREE floorplan available at the ticket desk. Outside the museum and in the pedestrian and cycle underpass under the museum there's often some sort of street entertainment, such as a 'living statue' on an old plinth that magically comes to life when someone puts a guilder in his hat. The museum also has a pleasant garden with statuary and fountains which is FREE to enter.

Sexmuseum Venustempel (Sex Museum) Damrak 18 (622 8376) *Open daily 1000–2330. Admission f8/E3.60.* Europe's only sex museum, a tacky, tawdry affair with risqué Indian and Far Eastern sculptures, Victorian sex films and objects and artworks from the Roman period to 1960.

Stedelijk Museum of Modern Art Paulus Potterstraat 13 (573 2911, www.stedelijk.nl) *Open daily 1100–1700. Admission f10/ E4.50.* One of Europe's most important museums for modern and contemporary art, this light and airy collection of over 1,000 Dutch and international art from 1850 onwards goes from impressionism and expressionism to pop and minimalism, and includes works by Picasso, Cézanne, Chagall, Matisse, Monet, De Kooning, Judd, Lichtenstein and Warhol, as well as photography, video and film, applied art and industrial design. The pictures by Kandinsky, Mondrian and Malewich very successfully show the origins of abstract art.

Tattoo Museum Oudezijds Achterburgwal 130 (625 1565, www.tattoomuseum.nl) *Open Tues–Sun 1200–1700. Admission f7.50/E3.40.* Housed in an old tobacco warehouse, the displays include a huge array of tools and illustrations through the ages and even preserved sections of tattooed skin.

Theatermuseum Herengracht 166–168 (551 3300) *Open Tues– Fri 1100–1700; Sat, Sun 1300–1700. Adults f7.50/E3.40, students f5/E2.25, 6–12s f2.50/E1.15.* Exhibits about the history of Dutch theatre, including a miniature theatre built in 1781, are housed in a beautiful 17th-century building with a splendid spiral staircase, extensive wall and ceiling paintings by Jacob de Wit and Isaac de Moucheron and ornate plasterwork. There is a tranquil garden where in the summer you can take tea.

Theo Thijssen 1e Leliedwarsstraat 16 (420 7119) *Open Thur– Sun 1200–1700. Admission f2.50/E1.15.* Manuscripts, first editions, photos, drawings, furniture and possessions of writer Thijssen.

Tropenmuseum (Tropical Museum) Linnaeusstraat 2 (568 8200, www.tropenmuseum.nl) *Open Mon, Wed–Fri 1000–1630; Tues 1000–2130; Sun 1200–1630. Adults f12.50/E5.65, children 6–17 f7.50/E3.40.* The Netherlands' largest ethnological museum, housed in an historic building. It has reconstructions of life in the tropics and subtropics, with walk-through displays recreating African and Asian streets. You can stroll around the yard of a Javanese house, wander through crowded Arab alleyways or get caught in a thunderstorm on the African savannah. There are also art exhibitions. The Kindermuseum (Children's Museum), geared to 6–12-year-olds, is next door (see separate entry, page 106).

Universiteitsmuseum de Agnietenkapel (University Museum Historical Collection) Oudezijds Voorburgwal 231 (525 3339) *Open Mon–Fri 0900–1700; closed 25–31 December and bank holidays. Admission FREE except during occasional special exhibitions.* Built in 1397, this splendid gothic chapel is one of Amsterdam's 17 medieval convents. It became part of the university when it was founded in 1632. There are temporary exhibitions about its history.

Vakbondsmuseum Henri Polaklaan 9, Plantage (624 1166) *Open Tues–Fri 1100–1700; Sun 1300–1700. Adults f5/E2.25, children f3/E1.35.* An exhibition about trade unions and the Dutch labour movement. The building itself is of interest, having been designed by influential Amsterdam architect H. P. Berlage in 1900, who considered it his finest work.

Van Gogh Museum Paulus Potterstraat 7 (570 5200, www.vangoghmuseum.nl) *Open daily 1000–1800. Adults f15.50/E7, 13–17s f5/E2.25, under-13s FREE.* Recently revamped, this very popular museum opened in 1973 contains a beautifully presented permanent exhibition including 200 paintings and 500 drawings by Van Gogh and his contemporaries such as Toulouse-Lautrec and Gauguin. The paintings are organised chronologically into five periods of Van Gogh's life: the Netherlands, Paris, Arles, Saint-Remy and Auvers-sur-Oise phases, and include a version of *Sunflowers, The Potato Eaters, The Yellow House in Arles* and the sinister *Wheatfield with Crows*, painted before his suicide in 1890.

Van Loon Museum Keizersgracht 672 (624 5255, www. musvloon.box.nl) *Open Mon, Fri–Sun 1100–1700. Admission f7.50/E3.40, under-12s FREE*. Descendants of influential merchant Willem Van Loon still own and look after this very well-preserved 17th-century house with 18th-century decor, lots of 17th–20th century portraits and splendid French gardens.

Verzetsmuseum (Museum of the Dutch Resistance) Plantage Kerklaan 61 (620 2535) *Open Tues–Fri 1100–1700; Sat, Sun 1200–1700. Adults f8/E3.60, 5–16s f5/E2.25*. This museum houses artefacts about the Dutch Resistance including a secret door to hide Jews, false identity papers, printing presses etc. Some exhibits are interactive.

Werf 't Kromhout Hoogte Kadijk 147 (627 6777) *Open Mon–Fri 1030–1600. Adults f4/E1.80, under-15s f2.50/E1.15*. Still a (just about) working shipyard, with a wharf covered in 1890 by two huge cast-iron roofs that is now a small nautical museum about early marine engineering, aiming to recapture the atmosphere of 19th-century shipbuilding.

Woonbootmuseum (Houseboat Museum) 'Hendrika Maria', Prinsengracht, moored opposite 296 (427 0750) *Open Tues–Sun 1100–1700. Adults f3.75/E1.70, children under 5ft (152cm) f2.50/E1.15*. This 90-year-old former commercial sailing boat has displays and a slide show about living on a houseboat. There are examples of interiors of houseboats on display.

Music

Information on and tickets for many music concerts are available from **AUB Ticketshop** Leidseplein 26 (0900 0191, from outside the Netherlands +31 20 621 1288, www.uitlijn.nl) *Open daily 0900–2100;* and **The Amsterdam Tourist Board** Stationplein, corner of Leidseplein/Leidsestraat (0900 400 4040, from outside the Netherlands +31 20 551 2525).

Admission to bars and cafés is generally FREE unless otherwise stated.

Akhnaton Nieuwezijdskolk 25 (624 3396) *Open Fri, Sat 1100–0400. Admission f10–f20/E4.50–9.* World music, including African and Latin American dance nights at this multi-storied centre which attracts a young pot-smoking crowd.

Alto Jazz Café Korte Leidsedwarstraat 115 (626 3249) *Open daily 2100–0300. Admission FREE.* A brown bar with live jazz and blues.

Arena 'S-Gravesandestraat 51 (694 7444) *Open Sun–Thur 2130–0200; Fri, Sat 2130–0400. Admission f10–17.50/E4.50–8.* A cultural centre in an ex-convent with generally underground acts usually on Friday nights.

Badcuyp Eerste Sweelinckstraat 10 A bar with different music each night, including a blues session on Tuesdays, salsa on Wednesday and jazz on Thursdays.

The Balmoral Nieuwe Doelenstraat 24 (554 0600) Scottish pub with live music on Wednesdays at 2100.

Bamboo Bar Lange Leidsedwarsstraat 66 (624 3993) *Open Sun–Thur 2000–0300; Fri, Sat 2100–0400. FREE admission.* Blues, jazz, pop, salsa and world music.

Barrel Organs Look out for the organ grinders, who still patrol the city with their *draaiorgels* (barrel organs), stopping every now and again to perform their version of 'Tulips from Amsterdam'.

Bethanienklooster Barndesteeg 6b (625 0078) This former monastery close to Nieuwmarkt has FREE recitals, from medieval works onwards, Fridays 1230–1330 except in the summer.

Beurs van Berlage Damrak 213 (627 0466) *Opening times vary. Admission from f15/E6.75.* Mainly classical concerts are held at this cultural centre.

Bimhuis Oude Schans 73–77 (631 1361, www.bimhuis.nl) *Opening times vary.* This venue has its finger on the pulse of the Dutch jazz scene, enjoying a typically mixed Dutch jazz audience ranging from under-20s to over-80s. You may get a classy clarinetist, or a 14-piece band fusing African percussion with European horns and electric guitar.

Bourbon Street Leidsekruisstraat 6–8 (623 3440) *Open Sun–Thur 2200–0400; Fri, Sat 2200–0500. Admission from f2.50/E1.15.* Live jazz, funk, blues, rock and roll.

Busking Vondelpark and Leidseplein have buskers (and street performers) but avoid the buskers of the tourist-sodden Rembrandtplein – unless you want to hear a tired old Dylan or Beatles track sung in a Dutch accent.

Café Nol Westeratraat 109 *Open Sun–Thur 2100–0300; Fri,*

Sat 2100–0400. Each night from about 2100 until late, there's accordion music, yodelling and a gigantic singalong of old Amsterdam songs at this sort of working man's club of the Jordaan. And it's FREE.

Carillons Amsterdam as a city has the most carillons in the world – nine in total. Most date from the 17th century and were built by the celebrated Francois and Pierre Hemony, who settled in Amsterdam in 1655. Hemony was the first bell-founder who knew exactly how to get the right note out of the bells. Four of these carillons give weekly FREE concerts: **Westertoren (the Western Tower)** *Tues 1200–1300;* **Zuidertoren (the South Tower)** *Thurs 1000–1100;* **the Muntto- ren (the Mint Tower)** *Fri 1200–1300;* **the Oudekerkstoren (the Old Church Tower)** *Sat 1600–1700.* Further details available from the Amsterdam Tourist Board.

Casablanca Zeedijk 26 (625 5685) *Open Sun–Thur 2000–0200; Fri, Sat 2200–0400. Admission FREE*. Live jazz Sunday to Wednesday evenings.

Club Arena s' Gravesandestraat 51 (694 7444, www.hotelarena.nl) *Open Thur 2300–0400; Fri, Sat 2300–0500. Admission f10/ E4.50 upwards*. Regular concerts.

Classical Music Recitals in Churches For details of FREE organ recitals and classical concerts being organised by the city churches, contact **The Amsterdam Uitburo, or AUB,** Leidseplein 26 (0900 01 91) *Open Fri–Wed 1000–1800; Thur 1000–2100*.

Concertgebouw Concertgebouwplein 2–6 (671 8345) *Admission from f10/E4.50*. A few classical performances at this major concert hall are inexpensive. The FREE lunchtime concerts on Wednesdays at 1230–1300 are especially popular but arrive early. They are held either in the Large Hall (Grote Zaal) or the Recital Room (Kleine Zaal). These concerts are often public rehearsals by orchestras, such as the Royal Concertbouw Orchestra, who will be playing to a paying audience in the evening. Sometimes there's jazz. From June to August these concerts are less frequent.

De Buurvrouw St Pieterpoortsteeg 9 (625 9654) *Open Sun–Thur 2100–0300; Fri–Sat 2100–0400. Admission FREE.* Some live rock music at this small bar.

De Engelbewaarder Kloveniersburgwal 59 (625 3772) *Open Mon–Sat 12.00–0100, Sun 1400–0100.* A popular bar with live jazz on Sunday afternoons.

De Koe Marnixstraat 381 (625 4482) FREE pop and rock concerts Sundays at 1600.

Engelse Kerk Begijnhof 48 (624 9665) *Admission FREE.* Weekly classical concerts and, in July and August, lunchtime concerts at this church located in the very attractive Begijnhof.

Gollem Raamsteeg 4 *Opening times vary.* There are around 200 beers as well as live music on Friday evenings at 1930.

Heeren van Amstel Thorbeckeplein 5 (620 2173) *Opening times vary.* Live jazz, pop or rock from around 2130.

Hoppe Spui 18–20 *Open Sun–Thur 0800–0100; Fri, Sat 0800–0200.* A brown café with live jazz on Monday evenings.

In de Wildeman Kolksteeg 3 *Open Mon–Sat 1200–0100; Sun*

1400–2100. Live traditional music at weekends in this popular beer bar.

In't Aepjen (The Monkey) Zeedijk 1 *Open daily 1500–0100.* On Saturday nights an acclaimed accordionist plays traditional Dutch ditties and sea shanties at this history-rich bar, and it's very popular with the locals.

Last Waterhole Oudezijds Armsteeg 12 (624 4814) Bar with live rock or blues on Friday and Saturday evenings at around 2200.

Maloe Melo Lijnbaansgracht 163 (420 4592, www. maloe melo.com) *Open Sun–Thur 2130–0200; Fri, Sat 2130–0300. Admission FREE.* Live blues, jazz, country and rock bands every evening from around 2300.

Melkweg Lijnbaansgracht 234a (531 8181, www.melkweg.nl) *Opening times vary. Admission and compulsory membership start from f10/E4.50.* As well as dance, theatre, art exhibitions and other cultural events, a variety of music performances are staged here.

Mulligans Amstel 100 *Open Mon–Thur 1600–0100; Fri 1600–0300; Sat 1400–0300; Sun 1400–0100.* Popular Irish pub with live music on Friday and Saturday evenings.

Muziektheater Waterlooplein 22 (625 5455) FREE hour-long classical recitals and 20th-century music, Tuesdays at 1230 in the Boekmanzaal, except usually during June–August.

Nieuwe Kerk Dam (626 8168) *Admission from f12.50/E5.65.* Regular organ recitals.

OCCII Amstelveensweg 134 (671 7778) *Open Sun–Thur 2100–*

0200; Fri, Sat 2100–0300. Admission approx. f10/E4.50. Local live bands.

O'Donnell's Ferdinand Bolstraat 5 (676 7786) *Open Sun–Thurs 1100–0100; Fri, Sat 1100–0300.* Irish pub with regular live Irish music.

O'Reilly's Paleisstraat 103 (624 9498) Irish pub with live Irish music.

Oude Kerk Oudekerksplein 23 (625 8284) *Admission from f7.50/ E3.40, concessions from f5/E2.25.* Choral concerts, chamber music and organ recitals at this imposing church.

Paradiso Weteringschans 6–8 (626 4521, www.paradiso.nl) *Opening times vary. Admission and compulsory membership start at f15/E6.75.* Anything from local bands to international acts, in a neo-Gothic church by Leidseplein.

Proust Noordermarkt 4 (623 9145) Modern café bar with live jazz/blues on Thursdays 2100, Sundays 1600.

Rock In and Roll Out Leidseplein 22 (421 5684) Touristy, but puts on live rock and roll and blues Tues–Fri.

Ronde Lutherse Kerk (Round Lutheran Church) Singel, corner of Kattengat. This baroque church holds FREE chamber music recitals on Sunday mornings.

Siberie Brouwersgracht 11 (623 5909) *Open daily 1100–2300.* This coffeeshop (i.e. cannabis joint) has regular live jazz evenings.

Stadhuis-Muziektheater Waterlooplein 22 Regular FREE classical music concerts on Tuesdays at 1230–1300, usually consisting of chamber music performed by the resident companies of the Musiektheater: the Netherlands Philhar-monic Orchestra, the Choir from the Dutch Opera and the Dutch Ballet Orchestra.

Stedelijk Museum of Modern Art Paulus Potterstraat 13 (573 2911, www. stedelijk.nl) Sometimes there are contemporary and experimental music concerts held here.

Tropenmuseum Tropeninstituut Theater, Linnaeusstraat 2 (568 8500) World music concerts.

Twee Zwaantjes Prinsengracht 114 (625 2729) *Open Sun–Thur 1000–0100; Fri, Sat 1000–0200*. On Friday and Saturday evenings this pleasant café bar decorated with stained glass has a singalong with old Amsterdam songs and accordion music as well as other regular live music evenings.

Van Puffelen Prinsengracht 377 (624 6270) *Open Sun–Thur 1500–0100; Fri, Sat 1800–2300*. Live jazz on Sundays at this spacious brown café.

VOC Café Schreierstoren, Prins Hendrikkade 94 (428 8291) *Open Mon–Thur 1000–0100; Fri, Sat 1000–0300; Sun 1200–2000*. A pleasant bar with terraces. There is regular live accordion and similar music.

Winston Kingdom Winston Hotel, Warmoesstraat 129 (623 1380, www.winston.nl) *Open Sun–Thur 2100–0230; Fri, Sat 2100–0300. Admission FREE to f10*. A wide mix of live music styles.

Zaal 100 De Wittenstraat 100 (688 0127) *Admission prices vary*. Regular jazz evenings and other music concerts.

Nightclubs

Apart from the red light district, nightlife is at its busiest on Rembrandtplein and Leidseplein. Leidseplein has the Stadsschouwburg, which is surrounded by cafés, small theatres, discos and cinemas. Rembrandtplein has discos, and restaurants and bars with large terraces. A weekly magazine, *Amsterdam This Week*, can give a good idea of the week's events and clubs worth visiting.

Arena 's-Gravensandestraat 51 (694 7444, www.hotelarena.nl) *Open Thur 2300–0400; Fri, Sat 2300–0500.* Large club at the Hotel Arena, with varied music selection including rock and house.

Café Meander Voetboogstraat 3 (625 8430, www.cafémeander. com) *Open Mon–Thur 2100–0300; Fri–Sun 2100–0400.* DJs play disco, jazz, funk and soul.

Café West Pacific Haarlemmersweg 8–10 (488 7778) *Opening times vary.* A café that becomes a club when it gets late, playing anything from funk to hip hop.

Dansen bij Jansen Handboogstraat 11 (620 1779, www.dansen bijjansen.nl) *Open Sun–Thur 2300–0400; Fri, Sat 2300–0500.* Well-established and inexpensive club for students.

Escape Rembrandtplein 11 (622 111, www.escape.nl) *Open Thur–Sun 2300–0400.* Huge club, often with queues.

Hotel Winston Warmoesstraat 123 (623 1380) *Opening times vary.* Café club playing a variety of music styles.

House of Soul Amstelstraat 32 (620 2333) *Open Thur–Sat 2300–0400*. Club for soul and funk lovers.

Industry Pardenstraat 17 *Open Thur, Sun 2300–0300; Fri, Sat 2300–0400*. Generally r&b is played at this club near Rembrandtplein.

iT Amstelstraat 24 (625 0111, www.it.nl) *Open Thur 2300–0400; Fri, Sat 2300–0500*. Rather camp and flamboyant club, with Saturday gay night.

Mazzo Rozengracht 114 (626 7500) *Open Wed–Sun 2300–0400*. A club to dance rather than pose at.

Melkweg Lijnbaanstraat 234 (624 1777) *Opening times vary*. Club nights every week.

Odeon Singel 460 (624 9711) *Open Sun–Thur 2200–0400; Fri, Sat 2200–0500*. Different music – such as r&b, hip hop and disco – on all three storeys.

Paradiso Weteringschans 6 (626 4521) *Opening times vary*. A concert hall that has regular weekend club nights.

Seymour Likely Nieuwezijds Voorburgwal 250 (627 1427) *Opening times vary*. Post-midnight hip nightclub and lounge bar.

Sinners in Heaven Wagenstraat 3–7 (620 1375, www.sinners.nl) *Open Thurs–Sun 2300–0400*. A club decked out in a dungeon theme, with choosy bouncers and three floors each playing different music, disco, house and hip hop. Drinks are expensive but entry is FREE before 2400.

Time Nieuwezijds Voorburgwal 163 *Opening times vary*. Music nights vary, including ragga, reggae, techno, house.

Trance Buddha Oudezijds Voorburgwal 216 *Open nightly 2300–*

0400. A must if you like trance music, with Buddhas over-looking the dancefloor.

Parks and Open Spaces

All are FREE to enter and open dawn to dusk, or longer, daily unless otherwise stated.

Amstelpark Europaboulevard Situated in the south-west sub-urb of Buitenveldert, this big park contains formal gardens, pony rides, a children's farm, rhododendron walk, mini-golf, mini-football, art exhibitions and a maze. At the southern tip is the Rieker windmill (built 1636). From April to October there is a miniature train.

Amsterdamse Bos (Amsterdam Woods) A 2,000-acre wood to get lost in with meadows and lakes where you can hire pedaloes and canoes. There are also playgrounds, bike hire from March to October, a horticultural and forestry museum (645 4575) *Open Mon—Sat 1100—1700, Sun 1300—1700, FREE admission*. There are also jogging/keep fit trails, a picnic area, summer open-air theatre, watersports centre, riding stables and a buffalo and bison reserve. There's even a goat farm (Bio Dyn Geitenkaasboerderij, tel. 645 5034) *Open Wed—Mon 1100—1700*. The visitors' centre is at Nieuwe Kalfjeslaan 4 (643 1414) *Open daily 1100—1700*.

Beatrixpark Boerenwetering pad One of the city's most attractive parks, it boasts a walled garden and children's play areas as well as a pond with herons and geese. There are concerts in the summer.

Flevopark Flevoweg Has a large expanse of woodland and meadow and two open-air swimming pools that are open in the summer.

Frankendael Gardens Middenweg 72 Tranquil, informal gardens with ancient trees, overgrown shrubs and nurseries. The ornamental facade of the 18th-century Louis XIV-style Frankendael House in the grounds can also be seen here.

Gaasperplas Park Gaasperplas A large lake, paddling pool and playground are just some of the attractions here.

Hortus Botanicus (Botanical Gardens) Plantage Middenlaan 2a (625 9021, www.hortus-botanicus.nl) *Open Apr–Oct Mon–Fri 0900–1700; Sat, Sun 1100–1600; Nov–Mar Mon–Fri 0900–1600; Sat, Sun 1100–1600. Apr–Oct adults f10/E4.50, under-15s f5/E2.25; Nov–Mar adults f7.50/E3.40, under-15s f4.50/E2.* Just to the east and a short walk from the bustling city centre, this tranquil retreat is one of the oldest botanical gardens in the world. It began in 1682 for cultivating medicinal herbs. More than 6,000 plant species are here, a number dating from that time. There are tropical, sub-tropical and desert greenhouses, a palm house containing the oldest potted plant, a 400-year-old cycad, a medicinal herb garden and an orangery, built in 1870, with a café and terrace that are perfect for afternoon tea.

Hortus Botanicus Vrije Universiteit Van der Boechorstraat 8, Zuid (444 9390) *Open Mon–Fri 0800–1630.* A small tranquil garden set between towering university and hospital buildings.

Oosterpark Mauritskade and 's Gravesandestraat This English-style park is good to combine with a visit to the nearby Tropenmuseum.

Rembrandtpark Postjesweg A large, lake-filled park west of centre.

Rijksmuseum Garden Stadhouderskade 42 (674 7047, www. rijksmuseum.nl) *Open daily 1100–1700*. Few visitors to the Rijksmuseum venture into its garden, which boasts mani-cured flowerbeds, summerhouses, sculptures and fountains. There's a hotch-potch of Dutch architectural ruins on show, which were gathered together from all over the Netherlands at the end of the 19th century. It evolved into a magnificent permanent exhibition featuring five centuries of Dutch architecture, which includes 17th-century city gates from Groningen and Deventer and Gothic pillars from Edam. The Fragmentengebouw (Fragment Building) is also worth seeing with its mish-mash of memorial stones, lion faces and festoons, all originating from 19th-century ruined buildings.

Sarphatipark Sarphatipark, Ceintuurbaan A small park with lots of grass and duck ponds south of De Pijp. It waas named after Dr Samuel Sarphati (1813–66) who did lots of good deeds for the city including founding schools and starting a waste-disposal service.

Vondelpark Vondelstraat/van Eeghenstraat Named after the 'Shakespeare of the Netherlands', Joost van den Vondel, this safe and friendly park right is in the centre of the city, a short walk from Museumplein. It has lakes, ponds, and cafés. Its 120 acres of lawns, waterways, rose gardens and meandering footpaths contain statues and monuments, as well as an animal enclosure known as 'the petting zoo', which is home to sheep, goats, llamas and parakeets. You'll often stumble across street entertainers and buskers, including jugglers, fire-eaters, musicians, break-dancers, astrologers and tarot and palm readers. I saw a man there juggling so many balls I couldn't count them, but maybe I'm just stupid. For refreshment there's 't Ronde Blauwe Theehuis (the round blue tea house), which was built in the 1930s and which resembles a flying saucer-cum-pagoda. There's also the Groot Melkhuis café on the northern side, which has a good children's playground. Vondelpark gets very busy in the summer and on Sundays, with kite-fliers, skaters and frisbee-throwers all adding to the atmosphere. Skaters can hire skates at a stand near the Amstelveenseweg entrance. There are loads of FREE events in the park from late May/early June through August as part of the Vondelpark Openluchttheater (673 1499, www.openluchttheatter.nl) season. These include theatre, children's shows, dance, classical and pop concerts, which take place most days in a wrought-iron music pavilion and a small ampitheatre on an island near the centre of the park.

Westerpark Westerpark A small park just west of the Jordaan neighbourhood.

Restaurants, Food Cafés, Tea Rooms and Other Eateries

The following establishments offer inexpensive food and at all you can obtain a meal or filling snack for under a fiver. Additionally, many of the *eetcafés* (pubs serving food) and grand cafés, some of which are mentioned in 'Cafés and Bars' (see page 56), offer excellent inexpensive meals and snacks.

Confusingly, unlike in Britain, in Amsterdam you go to a coffeeshop (see page 81) to smoke dope rather than to drink coffee. If you want a hit of caffeine, go to a coffee house (*koffiehuis*) or tea room.

There are a fair number of ethnic cafés in Amsterdam, which are part restaurant, part take away. You'll find a small room serving very authentic Turkish, Surinamese, Thai and Indonesian foods. Some are included here.

Indonesian food is especially prevalent in Amsterdam and indeed all over the Netherlands, because the 13,677 Spice Islands that now make up Indonesia were once the Dutch East Indies. If the price is right, try the *rijstafel* (rice table) to share, a banquet of dishes that could include satay, pork in coconut sauce with kmiri nuts, or chicken in sambal sauce. A cheaper alternative is *nasi rames*, where you get boiled rice with some of the accompaniments you'd get in a *rijstafel*. With noodles instead of rice this is *bami rames*.

The streets around Albert Cuypmarkt, the bustling general market in De Pijp, have lots of cheap little ethnic cafés and restaurants. The streets around Leidseplein, such as Lange Leidsedwarsstraat and Korte Leidsedwarsstraat, also have many restaurants, many catering for tourists. Snack bars and sandwich shops (*broodjeszaken*) are everywhere.

A popular lunch-time snack is *falafel*, essentially chick pea croquettes. There are falafel stores all over the city, and some of these are included here. Alternatively, try a dangerously addictive portion of Dutch-style chips (*frites* or *patat*), or the executive top-quality version, *vlaamse frites*, (i.e. Flemish fries), which come with mayonnaise, or sample the salted raw herring (*haring*) commonly sold on street stalls. Eel (*paling*), plaice (*schol*) and cod (*kabeljauw*) are also popular.

Other Dutch cuisine includes *erwtensoep*, a thick pea soup with smoked sausage and bacon; *kroketten* or *bitterballen*, deep-fried croquettes with meat, fish or shrimp, often served with mustard; *stamppot*, a mashed potato and vegetable stew served with pork or smoked sausage; *asperges*, white asparagus with butter and ham. *Uitsmijter* is a popular filling snack: a fried egg with meat, cheese and garnish.

The *dagmenu* or *dagschotel* (dish of the day) is often a good-value option, but don't count on it.

Cigarette smoking is still extremely popular in the Netherlands – unlike in America, where you're now virtually shot if you smoke in the street – so don't be surprised if you can't see your plate through the haze of tobacco smoke.

Albine Albert Cyuypstraat 69 (675 5135) *Open Tues–Sun 1030–2200*. An inexpensive restaurant near the Heineken Brewery serving Surinamese/Chinese food.

Al's Plaice Nieuwendijk 10 (427 4192) *Open Mon 1700–2200; Wed–Sun 1200–2200*. Cheap British-style chippie.

Anda Nugraha Waterlooplein 339 (626 6046) Inexpensive Indonesian.

Ankard Nieuwezijds Voorburgwal 16 (623 6110) *Open daily 1700–2400*. Excellent Turkish restaurant.

Arena 's Gravesandestraat 51 (694 7444) Café favoured by backpackers.

Axum Utrechtsedwarsstraat 85–87 (622 8389) Good-value Ethiopian.

Backstage Utrechtsedwarsstraat 67 *Open Mon–Sat 1000–1730*. A dinky little tea room where the toasted tuna sandwiches are highly recommended.

Bagels and Beans Ferdinand Bolstraat 70 (672 1610) *Open Mon–Fri 0830–1800; Sat 0930–1800; Sun 1000–1800*. Cheap good-quality breakfasts, light lunches and snacks.

Bakkerswinkel van Nineties Roelof Hartstraat 68 (662 3594) *Open Tues–Fri 0700–1800; Sat 0700–1700; Sun 1000–1600*. Bakery and tea room with sandwiches, soups etc from f6/ E2.72.

Balthazar's Keuken (Balthazar's Kitchen) Elandsgracht 108 (420 2114) *Open Wed–Fri 2000–2330*. A little restaurant with a few small wooden tables and a big kitchen just off the Prinsengracht canal. For the price of a pub meal you get wonderfully imaginative cooking, which could include anise pepperoni, cockles with parsley and ginger, or spinach poached in ouzo.

Bird Zeedijk 77 (420 6289). A little Thai snack bar, often crowded, with great, inexpensive food.

Bodega Keyzer Van Baerlestraat 96 (671 1441) *Open Mon–Sat 1200–1730*. Inexpensive Dutch cuisine.

Boerderij Meerzicht Koenenkade 56 (679 2744) Pancake house.

Bojo Lange Leidsedwarsstraat 51 (622 7434) *Open Mon–Fri 1600–0200; Sat, Sun 1200–0400*. Main courses start at f8/ E3.60 at this Indonesian eatery.

Bolhoed Prinsengracht 60 (626 1803) Good-value vegetarian/ vegan.

Brasserie Beethoven Beethovenstraat 43 (664 4816) *Open daily 1000–1800*. Features Dutch dishes.

Café Fonteyn Nieuwmarkt 13 (422 3599) *Open Sun–Thur 0930–0100; Fri, Sat 0930–0300*. Popular breakfast and light lunch joint.

Café Kalvertoren Singel 457 (427 3901) *Open Mon–Wed, Fri 0900–1800; Thur 0900–2100; Sat, Sun 1200–1800*. Café at the top of the Kalvertoren shopping centre with good views of the city.

Café-Restaurant Amsterdam Watertorenplein 6 (682 2666) *Open daily 1100–0100*. A huge ex-19th-century water pumping station away from the city centre.

Caffe Esprit Spui 10 (622 1967) Try the salads and sandwiches at this swish café.

Calzone Reguliersdwarsstraat 55–57 (627 3833) Inexpensive Italian.

Cambodja City Albert Cuypstraat 58–60 (671 4930) *Open Tues– Sun 1700–2200*. Main courses start at f12/E5.45 at this restaurant in the Pijp district serving Cambodian, Thai and Vietnamese food.

Caramba Lindengracht 342 (627 1188) South American fare.

Carmel Amstelveenseweg 224 (675 7636) Kosher cuisine.

Casa di David Singel 426 (624 5093) Cosy pizzeria.

Casa Juan Lindengracht 62 (623 7838) Tapas bar with very good Spanish food at reasonable prices.

De Bijenkorf (Beehive) Dam 1 (621 8080, www.bijenkorf.nl) This centrally located department store has a café or restaurant on each of its five floors.

De Blauwe Hollander Leidsekruisstraat 28 (623 3014) *Open daily 1700–2200*. A relatively inexpensive, dimly lit cosy restaurant with a small Dutch menu but the portions are generous. You may have to share a table but that is all part of the fun and it is an especially good restaurant in an otherwise very touristy district.

De Koperen Pan 1e Constantyn Huygensstraat 45 (683 9495) Dutch snacks and meals.

De Kroonprins Prins Hendrikkade 56 (622 8587) Inexpensive Dutch dishes.

Delice Leidsestraat 30 (627 6988) *Open daily from 0730*. Snacks.

De Nissen Rokin 95 (624 2825) Dutch snacks and meals.

De Roode Leeuw Damrak 93 (555 0666) A budget grill-room with Dutch specialities like *capucijners* which is broad beans, onions and bacon.

De Rozenboom Rozenboomsteeg 6 (622 5024) Dutch food.

De Vergulde Lantaarn Nieuwendijk 145 (624 5413) Dutch cuisine.

De Visscher Kalverstraat 122 (623 7337) *Open Fri–Wed*

1000–1900; Thur 1000–2130. Fast food including impressive fish meals.

De Vliegende Schotel Nieuwe Leliestraat 162–168 (625 2041) Inexpensive vegetarian dishes.

Duende Lindengracht 62, Jordaan (420 6692) *Open Sun–Thur 1600–0100; Fri, Sat 1600–0300.* Good-value *tapas* bar with Flamenco music.

Eat at Jo's Marnixstraat 409 (420 7469) *Open Wed–Sun 1400–2100.* Main courses from under f10/E4.50.

Eetcafé Loetfe Johannes Vermeerstraat 52 (662 8173) *Open Mon–Fri 1100–0100; Sat 1730–0100. A brown bar serving meals from f10/E4.50.*

Eetsalon van Dobben Korte Reguliersdwarsstraat 5–9 (624 4200) *Open Mon–Sat 0930–1800; Sun 1130–1800.* Sandwiches and snacks.

Egg Cream St Jacobstraat 19 (623 0575) A good, cheap pancake and vegetarian café.

Enorm PC Hoofstraat 87 (670 9944) *Open Mon–Fri 0800–2000; Sat, Sun 0900–1900.* An upmarket sandwich bar in the Museum Quarter.

Et Alors Nes 35 (421 6056) Cheap, unpretentious French food.

FEBO Numerous branches around the city Cheap fast food including chips with a variety of toppings.

Falafel Dan Ferdinand Bolstraat 126 (676 3411) *Open Sun–Thur 1200–0100; Fri, Sat 1200–0300.* Falafel, salads and an 'all you can eat' falafel fest from 1500 to 1700.

Falafel Maoz Regulierbreestraat 45 (624 9290) *Open Sun–Thur 1200–0100; Fri, Sat 1200–0300.* Falafel and salads.

Foodism Oude Leliestraat 8 (427 5103) *Open daily 1000–2200.* Friendly little café in the Jordaan with good-value breakfasts, snacks and lunches.

Gary's Muffins Prinsengracht 454 (420 1452) *Branches at Marnixstraat 121, Jodenbreestraat 15, Kalverstraat 185 (basement of American Book Center) and Regulierdwarsstraat 53. Open daily 0900–1800.* Good bagels, muffins, cookies, brownies and other snacks all baked on the premises, but few chairs.

Goodies Huidenstraat 9 (625 6122) *Open daily 0930–2230.* Bagels, sandwiches, pasta and other light meals.

Golden Temple Utrechtsestraat 126 (626 8560) Vegetarian/vegan.

Greenwoods Singel 103 (623 7071) *Open daily 1000–1900.* Muffins and cakes baked on the premises.

Grekas Singel 311 (620 3590) Takeaway/snack bar with good cheap Greek food.

Healthfood Restaurant De Bolhoed Prinsengracht 60–62 (626 1803) Organic vegetarian food.

Hein Berenstraat 20 (623 1048) *Open Wed–Mon 0900–1800.* Good-value breakfasts and lunches.

Hema Nieuwendijk 174 (623 4176) *Open Mon–Wed, Fri, Sat 1100–1700; Thur 1100–2000; Sun 1200–1600.* This department store near Centraal Station has a good cafeteria.

Het Badhuis Javaplein 21 (692 3483) International dishes.

Het Karbeel Warmoesstraat It may be in the red light district next to a sex shop, but this delightful café-restaurant, just a few minutes from Damrak, has very good-value meals, such as a mixed plate of meat and cheese for two for under a fiver.

Himalaya Warmoesstraat 56 (626 0899) *Open Mon 1300–1800; Tues–Sat 1000–1800*. New Age vegetarian/vegan café and tea room.

Hosokawa Max Eweplein 22 (638 8086) Japanese cuisine.

Indrapura Rembrandtplein 42 (623 7329) Indonesian food.

Ithaca Griekse Traiteur 1e Bloemdwarsstraat 18, Jordaan (638 4665) *Open Tues–Sun 1300–2200*. A small Greek restaurant.

J. G. Beune Haarlemmerdijk 156. A well-known tea room within a chocolate shop.

Kantjil and de Tijger Spuistraat 291 (620 0994) Indonesian: try the *rijstafel* (rice table), a bit of everything.

Keuken van 1870 Spuistraat 4 (624 8965) *Open Mon–Fri 1300–2000; Sat, Sun 1600–2100*. Classic Dutch food at this former soup kitchen near Centraal Station. Very good value.

KinderKookKafe Oudezijds Achterburgwal 193 (625 3257) *Times and costs vary, booking in advance essential*. This novel restaurant runs cookery courses for children and on Saturdays and Sundays the children run the whole show, cooking, serving and washing up. The simple meals are inexpensive.

Kismet Albert Cuypstraat 64. Delicious honeyed pastries, Turkish delight, stuffed peppers and mouthwatering Turkish stews.

Koffiehuis Dusart Dusartstraat 53 (671 2818) Coffee house and *eetcafé* in the Pijp, popular with locals.

Lalibela 1e Helmersstraat 249, Oud West (683 8332) *Open daily 1700–2300*. Just west of Vondelpark and Overtoom, this restaurant offers good Ethiopian food at low prices.

L'Angoletto Hemonystraat 18 (676 4182) *Open Sun–Fri 1800–2300*. A very popular and good authentic Italian trattoria.

Lanskroon Singel 385 (623 7743) *Open Tues–Fri 0800–1730*. Excellent patisserie.

Le Soleil Pancake House Niewe Spigelstraat 56 (622 7147) *Open daily 1000–2000*. Delicious pancakes from around £2 at this unpretentious pancake house on a delightful street.

Lime Zeedijk 104 (639 3020) *Open Tues–Thur 1700–0100; Fri 1700–0300; Sat 1200–0300; Sun 1200–0100*. Soups and sandwiches are just some of the fare at this café-bar.

Loekie Prinsengracht 705a (624 4230) *Open Mon–Sat 0900–1700*. Great sandwiches.

Meneer Pannekoek Readhuisstraat 6 (627 8500) Pancake bakery.

Metz and Co Café Keizersgracht 455 (520 7020) *Open Mon–Sat 0930–1730; Sun 1200–1700*. An ever-popular café in this famous department store, with a great view of the city. The brunches and afternoon teas are good value.

Moeder's Pot (Mother's Pot) Vinkenstraat 119, Jordaan (623 7643) *Open Mon–Sat 1700–2230*. Wholesome, basic Dutch food from f8/E3.60 per dish.

Mr Hot Potato Leidsestraat 44. Good baked potatoes, hamburgers, milkshakes, and interesting sandwiches such as roast pork with peanut satay sauce, lettuce and tomato.

Nam Kee Zeedijk 111–113, Old Centre (624 3470, www.namkee.nl) *Open daily 1200–2400.* A cheap and cheerful Chinese restaurant in the red light district.

Nielsen Berenstraat 19 (330 6006) *Open Tues–Sat 0800–1700; Sun 0900–1700.* Good-value breakfasts and lunches.

New York Bagels Buiten Oranjestraat 15 (639 3508) *Open Mon–Fri 0800–1800; Sat, Sun 1100–1700.* Bagels and other American-style snacks.

Oibibio Prins Hendrikkade 20–21 (553 9355) Near Centraal Station, a New Age café serving vegetarian dishes. It is within a complex housing a gym, restaurant, theatre and shop.

Old Nickel Nieuwebrugsteeg 11 (624 1912) Dutch food.

Pancake Bakery Prinsengracht 191 (625 1333) *Open daily 1200–2130.* This cosy and child-friendly pancake house with exposed brick walls and wooden beams on a very pleasant stretch of the Prinsengracht claims to bake the best pancakes in town (from f9.50/E4.30) and it's easy to believe. There are over 70 varieties and kids can draw with crayons while they're waiting

Pannekoekhuis Welcome Prinsengracht 358 (620 8448) Pancake house.

Pannenkoekenhuis Upstairs Grimburgwal 2 (626 5603) *Open Mon–Fri 1000–1900; Sat, Sun 1100–1700.* Tiny but good pancake house.

Pasta di Mamma P.C. Hoofstraat 52 (664 8314) Great selection of Italian cheeses and salads, or try *La Toscana*, virgin olive oil drizzled over bread, heaped with Parma ham, basil leaves and provolone cheese.

Piccolino Lange Leidsedwarsstraat 63 (623 1495) *Open daily 1200–2400*. Ever-popular, affordable Italian.

Pompadour Huidenstraat 12 (623 9554) *Open Tues–Sat 0930–1730*. Strikingly mirrored tea room.

Raan Phad Thai Kloveniersburgwal 18 (420 0665) Thai fast food.

Riaz Bilderdijkstraat 193 (683 6453) Cheap Surinamese food, such as curries with rice or *roti* (pancake).

Riebach Browersgracht 139 (626 7708) *Open Mon–Sat 0930–2200*. Good-value breakfasts and lunches.

Rose's Cantina Regulierswarsstraat 38 (625 9797) Tex-Mex food.

Sampurna Singel 498 (625 3264) Indonesian cuisine.

Say Satay Amstelstraat 26 (625 7560) *Open Sun–Thur 1700–2300; Fri, Sat 1700–0300*. It looks small from the outside, but inside this good-value Indonesian joint is both quite spacious and cosy.

Scaramouche Paleisstraat 15 (622 2043) Dutch food.

Smits Koffiehuis Stationplein 10 (623 3777) *Open daily 1000–2100*. An above-average vintage tea room near Amsterdam's Centraal train station.

Song Kwae Thai Food Kloveniersburgwal 14a (624 2568) Inexpensive Thai dishes.

Surinam Express Halvemaansteeg 18 (622 7405) An authentic Surinamese sandwich shop off Rembrandtplein with spicy curry fillings.

t'Balkje Kerkstraat 46 (622 0566) *Open daily 0900–1700.* Close to Leidsestraat, you can get inexpensive burgers, sandwiches and other snacks here.

Turquoise Wolvenstraat 22 (624 2026) Turkish *eetcafé* with inexpensive dishes.

Upstairs Grimburgwal 2 (626 5603) Pancakes.

Vennington Prinsenstraat 2 (625 9398) *Open Wed–Sat, Mon 0800–1600; Sun 1000–1600.* Trendy bagel and snack joint.

Villa Zeezicht Torensteeg 7 (626 7433) Eternally popular with students so it must be good value. Try the excellent apple pie.

Vlaams Friteshuis Voetboogstraat 31 *Open Mon–Sat 1100–1800; Sun 1200–1730.* Particularly good Dutch-style chips.

Vroom and Dreesman Kalverstraat 201 (622 0171) Large department store with a good cafeteria.

Walem Keizersgracht 449 (625 3544) *Open daily 1000–0100.* A modern, spacious bar with a summer garden and terrace overlooking the canal. Try the breakfasts and good-value toasted sandwiches.

Waroeng Asje Jan Pieter Heijestraat 180 (616 6589) An Indonesian takeaway with a few tables, near the Vondelpark. Try the *soto soep* – chicken and vegetable soup with rice.

Warung Spang-Makandra Gerard Doustraat 39 (670 5081) *Open Thur–Tues 1100–2200*. A cheaper Surinamese restaurant in the Pijp area.

Winkel Noordermarkt 43 (624 2938) *Open Mon–Sat 0800–1700*. This tea room is busiest on Mondays and Saturdays, which are Noordermarkt market days.

Zuivelhandel Hartman Hekelveld 6 (622 0672) *Open Mon–Fri 0730–1600*. Sandwiches and snacks.

Rollerskating and Rollerblading

On a freezing winter evening possibly under 100 skaters, and in summer maybe over 3,000, may participate in a mass three-hour skate every Friday evening through Vondelpark. It starts at 2000 near the Filmmuseum entrance.

Every July and August since 1997 there has been a very successful Tuesday night skate from 2000 outside Het Buitenhuis in Spaarnwoude, which is known as skaters' paradise, which is about 20km north of Amsterdam. Details are available on www.xs4all.nl/justb/skating/wheels/html.

Skaters participate in the **Delta Lloyd Amsterdam Marathon (663 0781, www.amsterdammarathon.nl)** *Mid-October*. Around 8,000 runners and skaters follow a 21-km trail twice through the city, through Vondelpark and the old city centre, starting and ending at the Olympic Stadium. The event has been held annually since 1975. There's music, dancing and various stalls near the stadium.

Balance Overtoom 464–466 (489 4723) *Open Mon 1300–1800;*
Tues, Wed, Fri 1000–1800; Thur 1000–2100; Sat 0930–1700.
Skate hire f17.50/E8 per day.

Rent A Skate Vondelpark 7 (06 5466 2262 mobile) *Open Apr–*
Oct Mon–Fri 1100–2130; Sat, Sun 1030–2000. Hire starts at
f7.50/E3.40 for an hour. The hire shop is situated next to
the café by the Amstelveenseweg.

Sex

Along with its attitude to soft drugs, Amsterdam's attitude
to sex is famously liberal, and the thriving sex industry is a
major earner for the city.

De Walletjes (the red light district) is one of Amsterdam's
oldest sections – it's situated to the left as you leave
Centraal Station. A triangle roughly bordered by Centraal
Station, the Dam and the Nieumarkt, de Walletjes (the
little walls) dates from the 14th century. Prostitution was
increasingly widespread at that time as more and more
sailors came to the city. Although this area is known as the
red light district of Amsterdam, there are others in the city.
However, this is by far the most widely known, the
splashes of neon signalling its existence.

Prostitution is legal and regulated. Around 5,000 prostitutes
work six- to eight-hour shifts here, pay tax on their earn-
ings, are members of their own trade union and undergo
frequent medical examinations.

This doesn't stop the area, however, which attracts over

100,000 people a night, being seedy and sleazy like any other red light zone. It's not for the faint-hearted, and all humanity is here, including a good helping of shady characters, pushers and junkies, and prostitutes trapped into debt and drugs. That said, the ambience is not particularly threatening, and the area has some of the most attractive architecture in Amsterdam.

If you do visit, call in on the helpful Prostitute Information Centre by the Oude Kerk, to get your bearings. You should not take photos of the window girls or loiterers unless you want a chance of your camera and head being smashed in. And don't enter into a conversation with a drug dealer.

Ironically, two of Amsterdam's most attractive streets, Oudezijds Achterburgwal and Oudezijds Voorburgwal, have shop-front windows filled with ladies posing under red neon lights. It is safe to walk through, but keep to the main thoroughfares and bury your wallet or purse.

Erotic Museum Oudezijds Achterburgwal 54 (624 7303) *Open Mon, Thur, Sun 1100–0100; Fri, Sat 1100–0200. Admission f5/E2.25.* Erotic sketches by John Lennon and a huge collection of sex toys.

Sexmuseum Venustempel (Sex Museum) Damrak 18 (622 8376) *Open daily 1000–2330. Admission f8/E3.60.* Europe's only sex museum, a tacky, tawdry affair with risqué Indian and Far Eastern sculptures and Victorian sex films.

Shops

Britons used to identikit high streets in the UK with the same old tired chains of shops will delight in the shopping and window shopping opportunities in Amsterdam. Gifts, clothes, furniture and much, much else that you would never see in Britain are here, often at prices substantially lower than you would expect in the UK.

There are shops specialising in almost everything under the sun, from coffins to condoms and hammocks to hashish. There are shops specialising in such things as cardboard boxes, toothbrushes, silk, Indonesian antiques, Spanish terracotta, clogs, 1950s household electrical goods, beers, whiskies, kites, wristwatches manufactured between 1920 and 1950, and Japanese kimonos. Many speciality shops are located at De Negen Straatjes, the Nine Alleys that crisscross the main canals.

FREE food is plentiful in the Dutch capital. Sample tastings at specialist food shops are a regular feature of life in the Netherlands and indeed it can be wise to try before you buy: if a Cheddar and Stilton ploughman's lunch is the extent of your cheese-tasting experiences, some of the more obscure Dutch cheeses may take some getting used to. And you may consider some Dutch liquorices either heavenly or as delicious as solidified diesel oil, depending on your taste buds.

For fashion, the most exclusive shopping streets are around Museumplein, especially P.C. Hoofstraat, Beethovenstraat, Hobbemastraat and van Baerlstraat. Behind the Royal

Palace on Dam Square, the Magna Plaza has been converted from a grand neo-Gothic post office into a luxurious shopping centre dominated by upmarket fashion boutiques.

If you do get homesick for the UK's familiar chains, a number are here too including Waterstones, Boots, Marks & Spencer and The Body Shop, all of which are along Kalverstraat, which is Amsterdam's answer to London's Oxford Street and on Saturdays and Sundays can be just as busy. It has department stores and a number of inexpensive chain stores and the Kalvertoren shopping centre. Nearby, on Nieuwendijk, there are clothes shops, souvenir shops and the Kolk shopping centre.

The Leidsestraat area has fashion boutiques, gift and souvenir shops as well as plenty of cafés if you need a rest from retail therapy. Other classic shopping streets include Damrak and Rokin.

The Museum District and Spiegelkwartier (Spiegel Quarter) contains many galleries and art and antique dealers offering furniture, glass, sculpture, clocks and curiosities. Check out Nieuwe Spiegelstraat especially. Art and antique lovers will also find art and antique dealers along the canals and around Rokin. In the Jordaan around the Elandsgracht there are also a number of antique dealers and galleries.

Aronson Antiquairs Nieuwe Spiegelstraat 39 (623 3103) Antique shop specialising in Delftware, Chinese porcelain and furniture.

Art Unlimited Keizergracht 510 (624 8419, www.artunlimited.nl) Apparently the biggest stock of postcards in Europe, so there's no excuse not writing home.

Astamangala Kerkstraat 168 (623 4402) The Himalayan ethnographical items are worth a browse.

Athenaeum Spui 14–16 (622 6248) Newsagent with the best choice of international publications, plus lots of interesting and unusual books.

Awareness Winkel Weteringschans 143 (638 1059) Environmentally friendly clothes.

BamBam Magna Plaza, Nieuwezijds Voorburgwal 182 (624 5215) Upmarket baby clothes shop.

Bell Tree Spiegelgracht 10 (625 8830) Near the Rijksmuseum, this established toy shop has a large range of interesting toys and games for all ages.

Bijleveld Nieuwe Spiegelstraat 45a (627 7774) Shop selling antique clocks.

The Body Shop Kalverstraat 157 (623 9789); Kinkerstraat 251 (683 7157); Nieuwendijk 196e (626 6135) Continental branches of the well-known British chain – here you can book a complimentary makeover.

C-Cecile Lijnbaansgracht 275 (624 7178) Dolls in Dutch costume, handmade jewellery and other souvenir items.

Condomerie Het Gulden Vlies (Condom Shop) Warmoesstraat 141 (627 4174, www.condomerie.com) A comparatively respectable little red light district shop with a huge variety of condoms including one which sings 'For He's a Jolly Good Fellow' at the crucial moment. In case you were wondering, there is a 'no fitting room' notice in the window.

De Bierkoning Paleistraat 125 (625 2336) Hundreds of beers.

De Bijenkorf (Beehive) Dam 1 (621 8080, www.bijenkorf.nl) Large, centrally located, comprehensively stocked fashionable department store on five floors, each with a café or restaurant.

De Kaaskamer Van Amsterdam (the Cheese Room of Amsterdam) Runstraat 7 (623 3483, www.echeese.nl) More than 300 cheeses both from the Netherlands and elsewhere, and other deli-type foods at this popular shop near Leidseplein. Try the Leiden, a Dutch cheese containing cumin seeds, which is a world away from the plastic-tasting cheese sold in British supermarkets.

Del Sur Nieuwezijds Voorburgwal 137 (622 7047) You can try some of the different olive oils sold here. See also Olivaria (page 150).

De Munt Vijzelstraat 1 (624 4533) A shop with a good selection of Dutch liquorices. It is by the Bloemenmarkt, the floating flowermarket.

De Ode Levantkade 51 (419 0882) Coffin shop with imaginative coffins such as the model that converts from a bookcase, and a rocket to launch the ashes into the sky.

De Speelmuis Elandsgracht 58 (638 5342) A traditional toy shop with miniature toys, dolls' houses, games and puzzles.

De Witte Tanden Winkel Runstraat 5 (623 3443) This specialist shop for toothcare products claims to have the world's largest collection of toothbrushes. Why not pick up a few cheap, original and easy-to-transport presents for the folks back home?

De Zeiling Ruysdaelstraat 21–23 (679 3817) Toy shop with wooden toys, puzzles, games and other traditional items.

Edward Kramer Nieuwe Spiegelstraat 64 (623 0832) Antique Dutch tiles and homewares.

Exota Hartenstraat 10 (620 9102) Stocks a good range of simple, stylish clothes and accessories including well-known brands and others which are far less so.

Exota Kids Nieuwe Leliestraat 32 A branch of the above, this is an upmarket kids' clothes shop.

Fifties-Sixties Huidenstraat 13 (623 2653) A little shop for nostalgia fans, full of authentic period pieces including working vacuum cleaners, lamps and toasters, as well as vintage pottery and the like.

Frozen Fountain Prinsengracht 629 (622 9375) Impressive designer furnishings, especially Italian and Scandinavian examples.

Galleria d'Arte Rinascimento Prinsengracht 170 (622 7509) A hunting ground for souvenirs, Delftware, ornaments and wall tiles.

Galerie KIS Paleisstraat 107 (620 9760) Loads of original non-mass-produced ideas for the home.

Gallery Steimer Reestraat 25 (624 4220) Jeweller Klaus Steimer's workbench is in the shop so you can see him at work.

Hajenius Rokin 92 (623 7494) Cigars, pipes, tobacco.

Head Shop Kloveniersburgwal 39 (624 9061) *Open Mon–Sat*

1100–1800. The 1960s origins of this shop devoted to the world of soft drugs are still apparent. It stocks such things as pipes, mushrooms and incense.

Hema Nieuwendijk 174 (638 9963) Department store: think Woolworths.

Holland Gallery De Munt Munttoren, Muntplein 12 (623 2271) Traditional tiles, decorated wooden boxes, Dutch-style dolls, antique Delftware and other souvenir goods.

Hooy and Co Kloveniersburgwal 10 (624 3014) Chemist shop dating from 1743.

Housewives on Fire Spuistraat 130 (422 1067) Worth inclusion for the name alone; visit it for both clothes and haircuts.

HP De Vreng En Zonen Nieuwendijk 75 In the corner of this wine and spirits supplier is a working *jenever* still and *oud jenever* is available in distinctive stone bottles. There's also an orange-coloured *jenever, Kus Me Snel* (Kiss Me Quick) or bright-green *Pruimpje Prik* (for matters of respectability the translation is not disclosed). The rafters contain more than 15,000 miniature bottles, the largest collection in the world.

Huize van Wely Beethovenstraat 72 (662 2009) Wonderful chocolate confections.

Jacob Hooij Kloveniersburgwal 12 (624 3041) Liquorice-lovers should head straight for this 18th-century shop, which sells the super-strong bitter Dutch variety served in traditional paper cones. If your taste buds can't stand it, try the sweeter variety. The shop also sells hundreds of herbs and spices, dispensed from earthenware jars and little wooden drawers.

Jacques Fijnaut Nieuwe Spiegelstraat 31 (625 6374) Antique shop specialising in Dutch 18th-century silver and international 18th-century furniture.

Joe's Vliegerwinkel Nieuwe Hoogstraat 19 (625 0139) Kites, boomerangs and yo-yos.

Jorge Cohen Edelsmith Singel 414 (623 8646) Cohen's art deco-inspired modern pieces use salvaged jewellery with new and old stones. The jewellers are happy to be asked questions about what they are currently working on.

Kitch Kitchen 23 Eerste Bloemdwaarstraat 183 (622 8261) If you want to deck out your home with lurid plastic woven shopping bags, tacky towel rails and bright plastic chandeliers, this is the place to come. It also has a children's section with colourful handmade Mexican toys.

Klompenboer (The Wooden Shoe Factory) Nieuwezijds Voorburgwal 20 (also entrance on Spuistraat) (623 0632, www.wooden shoefactory.com) Go to this authentic clog-making set-up for a pair of made-to-measure clogs, which are constructed on the antique lathe at the back of the shop. The shop features the largest selection of hand-crafted wooden footwear in Amsterdam and there is also a small collection of wooden shoes including miniatures and a pair that are over 700 years old.

Knuffels Nieuwe Hoogstraat 11 (427 3862) Toy shop with colourful mobiles, soft toys etc.

Koot Living Rozengracht 8–12 (626 5000) This is the place to go for unusual vases, bowls and jars made in materials such as stone, woven hessian or even suede.

Kunsthandel Frans Leidelmeijer Nieuwe Spiegelstraat 58 (625 4627) Antique outlet specialising in 1890–1940 decorative arts, with an emphasis on Dutch design.

Lady Day Hartenstraat 9 (623 5820) Great selection of vintage clothes.

Lambiek Kerkstraat 78 (626 7543) Comic books.

Laura Dols Wolvenstraat 7 (624 9066) Period clothing, especially from the 1940s and '50s.

Le Cellier Spuistraat 116 (638 6573) Large selection of beers, liqueurs and wines.

Maranon Hangmatten Singel 488–490 (420 7121) An amazing selection of hammocks.

Maison de Bonneterie Rokin 140 (531 3400) If you can't afford the clothes at this department store, admire the chandeliers and glass cupola.

Mechanisch Speelgoed Westerstraat 67 (638 1680) Traditional toys such as masks, jigsaws, wind-up toys and puppets.

Metz and Co Leidsestraat 34–36 (520 7020) Sumptuous shop dating from 1891 and owned by Liberty in London, selling furniture, fabrics, gifts and more.

Mr Kramer Reestraat 18–20 (626 5274) Crammed with antique dolls, with a cute doll hospital for convalescing cuddlies. Also a large collection of candles, candelabras and incense.

Nic Nic Gasthuismolensteeg 5 (622 8523) Furniture and furnishings from the 1940s, '50s and '60s.

Old Dutch Ceramics Nieuwendijk 24 (627 3974) Call in to see a demonstration of hand painting of Delft blue pottery.

Oldenburg Beethovenstraat 17 (662 5520) Wonderful collection of cakes, tarts, chocolates and other confectionery.

Olivaria Hazenstraat 2a (638 3552) The place to visit if you're an olive oil obsessive, this shop just deals in olive oils.

Outras Coisas Herenstraat 31 (625 7281) Great gift ideas, with a Mediterranean twist.

Patisserie Pompadour Huidenstraat 12 (623 9554) This little confectioner's and tea room, with an 18th-century Belgian interior, has marvellous handmade cakes, chocolates and pastries.

PGC Hagenhuis Rokin 92–96 (625 9985) Founded in 1826, this grand shop sells almost any cigar currently available, including the house brand as well as 20-inch Popeye-style clay pipes.

Pinokkio Magna Plaza, Nieuwezijds Voorburgwal 182 (622 8914) Kids' shop with Pinocchio dolls, rocking horses and wooden toys.

Prenatal Kalverstraat 40 (626 6392) A sort of Dutch Mothercare.

Puccini Bomboni Staalstraat 17 (626 5474); Singel 184 (427 8341) You can watch chocolates of all sizes being made at these pricey confectionery shops. There are some unusual recipes incorporating ingredients such as tea, thyme, honey and calvados.

Riena Herenstraat 32a (428 2390) North African, Middle Eastern and Asian lamps and gifts.

Riviere Maison Herenstraat 2–6 (622 7675) Baskets of flowers, candlesticks, cushions and lots of other goods.

Schaak en Go het Paard Haarlemmerdijk 147 (624 1171) Chess fanatics will like the wide range of chess sets available here.

Schaal Treinen Huis Bilderdijkstraat 94 (612 2670) New and vintage dolls' houses and vehicles, as well as model trains and kits to make model buildings.

Spiegelkwartier (Art and Antiques Centre) Nieuwe Spiegelstraat and Spiegelgracht Sandwiched between the Rijksmuseum and Herengracht, you can window-shop for Delft porcelain, antique tiles, clocks, watches, model boats, pipes and old portraits. On Saturdays the shop Shunyam sells pop art.

Storm Magna Plaza, Nieuwezijds Voorburgwal 182 (624 1074). Children's designer clothes store.

Stout Berenstraat 9 (620 1676, www.meisjes.net) A perhaps inappropriately named, elegant lingerie shop.

3-D Hologrammen Grimburgwal 2 (624 7225) Gallery of holograms.

Van Tetterode Singel 163 (620 6382) Established 1919, this shop sells glass *objets d'art*.

Vroom and Dreesman Kalverstraat 201 (622 0171) One of a chain of department stores with a good cafeteria.

Water Shop Roelof Hartstaat 10 (675 5932) Over 100 kinds of bottled water from all corners of the world are for sale here as well as a wide variety of glassware.

Wegewijs Kaas and Deli Rosengracht 32, Jordaan (624 4093) An authentic Dutch cheesemaking outfit run by the Wegewijs family for over a century. You can sample some of over 160 Dutch and foreign cheeses.

Wonen 2000 Rozengracht 219, 223 (521 8710) Inspiring furniture and houseware by Dutch and international designers.

Zipper Huidenstraat 7 (623 7302) A good selection of vintage clothes, especially those from the 1970s and '80s.

Sightseeing and Places of Interest

Admission is *free* unless otherwise stated.

Amstelsluizen by Amstel 115 This row of 18th-century wooden sluice gates across the Amstel river are used four times a week in summer and twice a week in winter to stop the city's canals from stagnating. The gates are closed to allow fresh water to enter the canals, while sluices west of the city are opened to let the old water flow into the North Sea. The sluice gates are located next to the intricately decorated classical facade of the Koninklijk Theater Carre, built in 1887.

Beurs van Berlage (Stock Exchange) Damrak 277; entrance at Beursplein 1 (530 4141) *Open (museum) Tues–Sun 1000–1600. Adult f7/E3.15, child f4/E1.80.* Amsterdam's stock exchange, built 1897, is an architectural monument with an exhibition centre and museum, two concert halls, a café and restaurant. You can climb the adjoining open-air tower.

Bloemenmarkt (Flower Market) Singel, between Muntplein and Koningsplein *Open Mon–Sat 0930–1700.* Many visitors to Amsterdam are a tad disappointed by this, the world's only floating flower market, which is no more than a row of 15 permanently moored barges. Although it contains some pretty floral displays, on a rainy day it can more resemble a Wolverhampton garden centre than fields of Dutch tulips. Still, the market, which began in 1862, boasts a huge selection of plants, herbs and bulbs including rare black tulips, bulbs from Easter Island and indoor cypresses.

Bridges Amsterdam has nearly 1,500 bridges. Where Keizersgracht meets Reguliersgracht you can see seven of them running parallel, and where the Reguliersgracht crosses the Herengracht on the uneven numbered side there is a bridge from which you can see 15 others. Stand on that bridge and you will see six in a row. On the left-hand side of the Herengracht you'll see another six and on your right another two. You're standing on the 15th. At night they are all illuminated with hundreds of little lights. One of Amsterdam's bridges, the 17th-century Magerebrug (Skinny Bridge) linking Kerkstraat and Nieuwekerkstraat is, uniquely, made from wood and has to be repaired every 20 years. The Blaubrug (Blue Bridge) along the Amstel is not blue but made of stone, but the original wooden bridge here in the 17th century may have been painted blue. The Blaubrug features sculptures of fish, medieval boats and the Amsterdam crown.

Canals Unless you're a sex or dope addict, possibly the best thing about Amsterdam is its gorgeous canals. One of the most pleasant ways to spend a warm evening is simply to stroll along the tree-lined canal banks. The best canals are the concentric Prinsengracht, Keizersgracht and Herengracht, which are notable for the stunning 17th- and 18th-century houses lining them. At the Golden Curve area south-west of the city centre, at the bridge at the crossing of the Reguliersgracht with the Herengracht, you can see 15 bridges at once.

Centraal Station Stationplein Few train stations around the world deserve a second look, but this is one of them. Designed by architect J. H. Cuypers, who also designed the Rijksmuseum, and with which it shares similarities, it was completed in 1889 and boasts two towers adorned by a clock and a wind-rose, as well as classically inspired reliefs.

Dam Square This is where Amsterdam began, in that a dam was built by fishermen to separate the IJ from the Amstel. Around it are the streets that make up the medieval centre of the city. Schrieierstoren, opposite the imposing 19th-century Centraal Station, used to be a section of the old town wall.

De Krijtberg Singel 442–448 (623 1923) *Open for church services only, Mon–Fri 0815, 0930, 1230, 1745; Sat 1715; Sun 0800, 0930, 1100, 1230, 1715.* With its tall, narrow facade dwarfing the dainty canal houses beside it, this very impressive twin-steepled neo-Gothic church really captures the spirit of Amsterdam. It was built in the place of three houses and a clandestine Jesuit church in 1884 and has a bright, ornate interior.

Effectenbeurs (Stock Exchange) Beursplein 5 (550 4444) Built in 1913 by Pierre Cuypers of Rijksmuseum fame. Groups can phone to book a FREE guided tour of the stock, options and commodity exchange.

Felix Meritis Building Keizersgracht 324 (626 2321) Designed by Jacob Otten Husly and completed in 1778, this neo-classical building sports an impressive Palladian facade and was originally a science and arts centre, becoming Amsterdam's main cultural centre during the 19th century. The Dutch Communist Party occupied the building after World War II but it returned to its artistic cultural roots in the 1970s and now stages theatre productions and artistic events. It is best viewed from the opposite side of the canal.

Ferry Ride Young children love the ferry ride over the IJ beginning behind Centraal Station, the oldest part of Amsterdam's port. Although this trip to north Amsterdam only lasts a few minutes, there are splendid views of the shipping, the banks of the IJ and the expanse of water. There's little of interest directly on the other side, but about three miles on there's good countryside. The ferry, the 'Buikersloterwegveer', leaves landing stage 7 behind Centraal Station (de Ruijterkade) every 5–10 minutes or so, night and day. A smaller ferry, the 'IJ-Veer', leaves from landing stage 8 and transports passengers to a more easterly point on the northern bank of the IJ, but this ferry only runs Mon–Fri, 0635–1805.

Gable Stones As you walk around the city you will often see a gable stone (*gevelstenen*) about halfway up the wall with a name, a statue in relief or maybe a proverb. Until the end of the 18th century, these gable stones were used to show who lived in the house and the trade or profession they followed. They also served as the address. They could be very imaginative: at Lindengracht 55, for example, is a gable stone depicting 'the world turned upside down', with fish swimming in the tree and the name spelled backwards. The Jordaan has many gable stones, and you can see loaves of bread for bakers, pigs and sheep for butchers and breast-feeding women for wet nurses. These stones were discontinued after 1795 when Napoleon introduced a system of house numbers and street names.

Haarlemmerbuurt (Haarlem Quarter) Haarlem, just north-west of Centraal Station and by the Jordaan, is seldom included in visitors' itineraries yet it shows what central Amsterdam is like without tourists. Along Haarlemmer-straat, by the Herenmarkt, a tranquil upmarket residential area, is the Westindisch Huis, which in 1623 was home of the West India Company. Haarlemmerpoort (Haarlem Gate) on Haarlemmerplein dates from 1840. A walk by the pretty Brouwersgracht (Brewers' Canal) here reveals a whole row of former warehouses running from numbers 172 to 212.

Holland Experience Waterlooplein 17 (422 2233, www.holland-experience.nl) *Open daily 1000–1800. Adults f17.50/E7.90; under-16s, over-65s f15/E6.75.* A touristy enterprise where you sit on a moving platform in an aircraft-style seat, put on a pair of 3D glasses and take a trip through the Netherlands and all its clichés including windmills, clogs, dykes and tulips. You take a sub-virtual trip through the harbour of Rotterdam, the Keukenhof (bulbfields in Lisse) and Maurodam.

Hollandsche Manege Vondelstraat 140 (618 0942) *Open Mon 1400–2400; Tues–Fri 1000–2400; Sat, Sun, 1000–1800.* This little-known neoclassical gem is the Netherlands' oldest riding school and was inspired by Vienna's celebrated Spanish Riding School. At its café you can watch the lessons and enjoy its beautiful interior. A few doors away is a church, the Vondelkerk, designed by Pierre Cuypers and completed in 1880, and the greenery of Vondelpark.

Homomonument Westermarkt. Three triangles of pink granite forming a larger triangle, the Homomonument is the globe's first memorial to persecuted gays and lesbians. From June to August, 1200–1800 daily, an adjacent kiosk stocks information including FREE magazines and maps, all geared to gay visitors.

Koninklijk Paleis (Royal Palace) Dam Square - (624 8698, www.kon-paleisamsterdam.nl) *Open June–Aug daily 1200–1700; Sept–May days vary, 1230–1700. Adults f8/E3.60; 5–16s f6/ E2.70.* Designed by Jacob van Campen in the 17th century, and originally the city hall before becoming a palace when French Emperor Louis Napoleon converted it into one in 1808, this imposing building rests on over 13,000 wooden piles embedded in the sand below. There is a rich variety of sculptures in the galleries and other halls. The huge Citizen's Hall is decorated in marble and bronze and there are chimney pieces painted by Bol and Flinck, pupils of Rembrandt. The 'Vierschaar', the room where death sentences were pronounced until the 18th century, is also impressive. Guided tours are available.

Leidseplein A main tourist centre of the city, Amsterdam's liveliest square and tram intersection has buskers and street performers including fire eaters, jugglers and acrobats, and in the winter sometimes a free open-air ice rink. The buskers tend to be of a higher standard than those in residence at the even more tourist-sodden Rembrandtplein, but its fast food cafés hardly convey much Dutch flavour in the way they did in years gone by. Leidseplein has always been one of the busiest areas of Amsterdam: in the 17th century visitors to the city left their horses and carts here. Its name originates from the huge city gate demolished in 1862, the Leidsepoort.

Madame Tussauds Scenerama Dam 20 (622 9239, www.madame-tussauds.com) *Open daily 1000–1730. Adults f19.95/E9.00, children 5–16 f16/E7.20.* Wax museum comprising local and international celebrities rubbing shoulders with the Dutch royal family. Special effects and moving wax figures also attempt to create what life was like in Holland's Golden Age.

Magerebrug (Skinny Bridge) Links Kerkstraat and Nieuwekerkstraat. One of Amsterdam's more interesting bridges, originally built 1671 and uniquely made from wood, meaning that it has to be repaired every 20 years. It is still operated by hand, and if you stand in the middle it rocks with the traffic.

Max Euwe Centrum Max Euweplein 30A, off Leidseplein (625 7017, www.maxeuwe.nl) *Open Tues–Fri and first Sat of month 1030–1600.* Chess lovers will enjoy this homage to the Netherlands' only world chess champion Euwe. You can play against chess computers or real people, and there is an international library and various artefacts relating to chess. Enthusiasts of the game also hang out at **Schaakcafé** (see entry page 73) and there's a shop specialising in chess sets, Schaak en Go het Paard (see entry page 73).

Montelbaanstoren Oude Waal/Oude Schans 2 A medieval tower. The lower section was built in 1512 and was part of the city's medieval fortifications. The octagonal section and timber steeple were added in 1606. The Montelbaanstoren features in some of Rembrandt's etchings.

Moses en Aaronkerk Waterlooplein 205 (622 1305) *Open for exhibitions only*. Designed by Flemish architect T. Suys the Elder in 1841, this church features twin wooden towers.

Muiderpoort Alexanderplein Designed by Cornelius Rauws in 1770, this former city gate features a grand dome and clock tower above Doric columns.

Munttoren (Mint Tower) Muntplein This medieval tower that looms over the floating flower market on the Singel canal was part of the 15th-century Regulierspoort, a city gate that burned down in 1619. The tower was built in 1672 on what remained. The national mint used to be here. The tower is floodlit at night and a carillon usually plays for 15 minutes from 1200.

Nationaal Monument Dam This 22-metre (70ft) white obelisk was erected in 1956 in honour of the Dutch servicemen who died in World War II. It was designed by J. J. P. Oud and incorporates sculptures by John Raedecker. Eleven of the urns contain soil collected from the Dutch provinces existing at the time and the 12th contains earth taken from war cemeteries in Indonesia, which was a Dutch colony until 1949. The statues symbolise war (the four men), peace (the woman with a child) and resistance (the men and dogs).

Nieuwe Kerk (New Church) Dam (626 8168, www.nieuwekerk.nl) *Opening times vary. Admission is FREE or varies.* The church is 'new' in the sense that it was built in 1408 (as opposed to the Oude Kerk – Old Church – in the red light district, which was built a century earlier). It is now used for recitals, art exhibitions and state occasions – every Dutch monarch has been crowned here since 1815 – rather than as a place of worship. Despite damage and restoration caused by fires in 1421, 1452 and 1645, there's plenty to admire: an intricately carved pulpit, splendid organ, stained-glass windows and tombs of various local eminent people. The sundial on the tower was used to set all the clocks in the city until 1890.

Nieuwmarkt This open, paved square by the red light district is dominated by the Waag (see page 164). It evolved into a marketplace in the 15th century and today still hosts an antiques market. It contains a variety of pretty 17th- and 18th-century gabled houses.

Noorderkerk (North Church) Noordermarkt This church by the Prinsengracht canal was designed by Hendrick de Keyser and completed in 1623. It was built for the Jordaan's 'common people', while the posh punters attended the Westerkerk.

Normaal Amsterdams Peil (Normal Amsterdam Level) In the passage between the town hall and the music theatre on Waterlooplein is the Normal Amsterdam Level (also known as the NAP), a measuring point that is the standard from which water levels from a number of other countries in Europe are measured. Alongside the bronze button representing the exact NAP, three other glass columns rise out of the floor. The water in two of these columns indicates the present water level of the sea at Flushing and at IJmuiden. The water level in the third column bubbles almost five metres above your head and is the exact height the sea water reached during the dreadful floods in Zeeland in 1953.

Oostindisch Huis Oude Hoogstraat 24 Now part of the University of Amsterdam, this austere building dating from 1605 used to be the headquarters of the Dutch East India Company. Although much the interior decoration is gone, the exterior is a good example of an early 17th-century facade.

Oude Kerk (Old Church) Oudekerksplein 1 (625 8284, www.oudekerk.nl) *Open Apr–Nov Mon–Sat 1100–1700, Sun 1300–1700; Dec–Mar Sun–Fri 1300–1700. Admission f7.50/ E3.40.* This church is located in the heart of the red light district, perhaps not the best surroundings for the oldest surviving building in Amsterdam. The original wooden church was built in 1306 in the Brabant-style Gothic and was greatly altered during the following 300 years. Unusually, nearly all the roofs are the medieval originals, and there are 16th-century stained-glass windows and a notable Renaissance facade above the northern portal. The church has a very impressive Muller organ dating from 1724. Some of the carvings on the choir stalls could be described as rude, but then this is Amsterdam. The church has a beautiful tower with the city's oldest bell (1450) and a 47-bell carillon dating from 1658.

Pintohuis Sint Antoniesbreestraat 69 (624 3184) *Open Mon, Wed 1400–2000; Fri 1400–1700; some Sats 1100–1400.* Now a public library, the Pintohuis is so named because it was bought in 1651 by the rich Portuguse merchant Isaac de Pinto. His reworked Italianate design features a facade with six magnificent pilasters and inside the ornate ceilings are decorated with cherubs and birds.

Poezenboot (Cat Boat) moored opposite Singel 40 (625 8794) *Opening times vary.* Cat lovers will enjoy a trip here. Henriette van Weelde has been caring for Amsterdam's stray cats for over 25 years and visitors can see dozens (usually around 70) sprawled all over her canalboat. If cats are your thing, also take a trip to the Kattenkabinet (Cat Cabinet) at Herengracht 468, a gallery of artworks featuring cats.

Portuguese-Israelite Synagogue Mr Visserplein 3 (624 5351, www.esnoga.com) *Open Apr–Oct Mon–Fri, Sun 1000–1600; Nov–Mar Mon–Thur 1000–1600, Fri 1000–1500. Adults f7.50/E3.40; 10–15s f5/E2.25.* Located in the old Jewish quarter, this impressive candlelit synagogue built between 1671 and 1675 and restored after the war is open to all. London's oldest synagogue, at Bevis Marks and built in 1701, copied it in every detail. South of the synagogue is a square, Jonas Daniel Meijerplein, named after the Netherlands' first Jewish lawyer. On the square can be seen the Dockworker statue, by Mari Andriessen in 1952, commemorating the dockworkers' general strike in 1941 in protest at the treatment of Jews.

Rembrandtplein Although this area has largely degenerated into a tacky tourist trap of dreary cafés, bars, peep shows and striptease joints and restaurants, the art deco Tuschinski cinema (see page 164) survives and the grand De Kroon café has more going for it than most. The square held a butter market until the mid-19th century and until 1876 it was called Reguliersmarkt. It was renamed in honour of Rembrandt, and Amsterdam's oldest statue of him, in the centre of the gardens, was erected in the same year. Soon after a number of hotels and restaurants opened, including the Schiller Karena Hotel and the Café Schiller in 1892.

Ronde Lutherse Kerk (Round Lutheran Church) Singel, corner of Kattengat. Built in 1668–71 to replace the old one on Spui Square, this baroque church is the only circular Protestant church in the Netherlands. It holds FREE chamber music recitals on Sunday mornings.

Scheepvaarthuis (Shipping House) Prins Hendrikkade 108 This imposing building was built in 1916 and is considered the first example of the Amsterdam School of architecture. It features stained-glass skylights, staircases, doors, windows and interior walls decorated with nautical images.

Schipholscoop Arrivals Hall 1, Schiphol Airport, Zuid (601 2000) *Open Mon–Fri 1100–1700; Sat, Sun 1200–1700. FREE. Rail: Schiphol Airport.* If you're waiting for a plane, this visitors' centre has interactive displays about the airport and related matters.

Schreierstoren Prins Hendrikkasde, corner of Geldersekade East of the Zeedijk at the tip of the canal stands this little brick tower that used to be part of Amsterdam's fortifications. Dating from 1480, it is the oldest such tower in existence.

Schuttersgallerij (Civil Guards Gallery) Kalverstraat 92 (523

1822, www.ahm.nl) *Open Mon–Fri 1100–1700; Sat, Sun 1100–1700*. This exhibition is at the entrance to the Amsterdams Historisch Museum (Amsterdam Historical Museum). Walk through the small historic gate of the Municipal Orphanage to the only street in the world where paintings hang on the wall (the street is covered, naturally). There are 15 magnificent 16th- and 17th-century oil paintings of the civil guards. The most famous of these paintings is Rembrandt's *Nightwatch*, which draws huge crowds elsewhere at the Rijksmuseum. Also, the museum's café houses a wooden statue of Goliath which is over five metres high.

Sint Nicolaaskerk Prince Hendrikkade 76, by Centraal Station (624 8749) *Open Easter–Oct Mon 1330–1600, Tues–Sat 1100–1600; Nov–Mar Sun 1000–1400*. A neo-Renaissance church built in 1885 which has a dark interior.

Tuschinskitheater (Tuschinski Cinema) Reguliersbreestraat 26–28 (626 2633) Built in 1921 by Albert Tuschinski, a refugee from Polish pogroms, this magnificent art deco blended with Amsterdam School ex–variety theatre has been well preserved, and is a sea of bright murals, coloured lights, gaudy carpets and wrought iron. For the detailed low-down, book a guided tour on Sunday and Monday mornings (f10/E4.50 for adults and children).

Waag (Weigh House) Nieuwemarkt 4 Constructed in 1488, the multi-turreted Waag was originally known as St Anthoniespoort (St Anthony's Gate) and was part of the city's fortifications. In 1617 it became the city's public weigh house and citizens would have their produce weighed here and taxed. It has since been used for public executions and has been a fire station, a store for the city archives and a museum, before ending up today as a restaurant.

Westelijke Eilanden (Western Islands) Despite being less than a kilometre west of Centraal Station and north of Jordaan, few visitors to Amsterdam venture to the Western Islands built into the IJ. Yet it's worth a stroll, past the many warehouses now converted to homes and artists' studios. A narrow bridge links the prettiest two islands, Realeneiland and Prinseneiland. Note the 17th-century sand market, Zandhoek, located on the eastern waterfront of Realeneiland.

Westerkerk (West Church) Prinsengracht 279/Westermarkt (624 7766, tower 552 4169) *Open: church Apr–Aug Mon–Fri 1100–1500; Jun–Aug Sat 1100–1500; tower Apr–Aug Mon–Sat 1100–1700. Admission: church FREE, tower f3/E1.35.* This neoclassical church in the Jordaan district was built in 1631 and sports an 85-metre-high (276ft) tower, the highest in Amsterdam, which delivers a great view of the city, though it's a strenuous climb. The tower sways more than an inch in a strong wind (but there's no extra charge for this). Rembrandt is buried beneath the church (although no-one seems to know exactly where).

Zuiderkerk (South Church) St Antoniebreestraat 130–132 (689 2565) *Open: tower June–Sept, Wed–Sat 1400, 1500, 1600; church Mon–Wed, Fri 1200–1700, Thur 1200–2000. Admission tower f3/E1.35 for adults and children; church FREE.* The former graveyard of this Protestant church designed by Hendrick de Keyser and completed in 1611 is now a peaceful square. In the summer you can climb the tower for a bird's eye view of central Amsterdam. The church ceased to hold services in 1929. In World War II it was used as a morgue and now it is home to the Centre for Planning and Public Housing (622 2962), and has exhibitions on urban planning. If you have the time, call in briefly at St Anthoniesbreestraat 69 which is the Pintohuis, now part of a library, to see the beautiful ceilings.

Swimming

Bijlmersportcentrum Bijlmerpark 76, Bijlmer (697 2501) *Opening times vary. Adults f5.25/E2.40; children f4.75/E2.15.* Indoor and outdoor pools.

Bredhuisbad Spaarndammerdijk 306 (682 9116) *Open May–Sept daily 1000–1700.* Outdoor pool north-west of the city centre.

Flevoparkbad Zeeburgerdijk 630, Oost (692 5030) *Open May until first week of Sept daily 1100–1700 or later in hot weather. Adults and children f4.75/E2.15; concessions f4.50/E2.* East of the city centre, this complex has two large open-air swimming pools and a playground.

Floraparkbad Sneeuwbalweg 5 (632 9030) *Opening times vary. Adults f6.35/E2.85; children f5.30/E2.15.* Indoor and outdoor pools north of the city centre.

Jan van Galenbad Jan van Galenstraat 315 (625 4843) *Open May–Aug, times vary.* Outdoor pool to the west of the centre.

Marnixbad Marnixplein 5–9, Jordaan (625 4843) *Open daily, times vary. Adults f4.75/E2.15, children f4/E1.80.* Indoor pool with slides etc, at the west side of Westerstraat.

Mirandabad De Mirandalaan 9 (622 8080/642 8080, www. mirandabad.nl) *Open Mon–Fri 0700–2200; Sat, Sun 0930– 1700. Adults and children f6.50/E3.* Indoor and outdoor pools south of the city centre. Amenities include a tropical-style pool with slides, 'beach', wave machine and whirlpool.

Sloterparkbad Slotermeerlaan 2 (613 3700) *Adults and children f5/E2.25.* Indoor and outdoor pools, west of the centre near the tram 14 terminus.

Theatre, Dance, Opera, Live Comedy

Information on and tickets for theatre performances (as well as music concerts) is available from: **AUB Ticketshop** Leidseplein 26 (0900 0191, from outside The Netherlands dial +31 20 621 1288, www.uitlijn.nl) *Open daily 0900–2100;* **The Amsterdam Tourist Office,** Stationplein, corner of Leidseplein/ Leidsestraat (0900 400 4040, from outside The Netherlands +31 20 551 2525).

Badhuis Theater de Bochel Andreas Bonnstraat 28 (668 5102) *Admission f7.50/E3.40 to f15/E6.75.* Children's shows and workshops.

Bellevue Leidsekade 90 (530 5301, www.theaterbellevue.nl) *Admission from f17.50/E8.* Theatre and cabaret.

Boom Chicago Leidseplein 12 (423 0101, www.boomchicago.nl)

Admission from f15/E6.75. Improvised comedy and stand-up theatre satirising Amsterdam life which is eternally popular with locals and tourists alike.

Circustheater Elleboog Passeerdersgracht 32 (626 9370) *Opening times vary. F15/E6.75 per day.* Children aged 4–17 can learn circus skills here, whether tightrope walking, clowning, balancing or juggling. Teachers speak English and family and friends can attend a circus performance at the end of the session, which costs f15/E6.75 for adults, and f10/E4.50 for under-17s.

Comedy Café Amsterdam Max Euweplein 43 (638 3971, www.comedycafe.nl) *Admission prices vary. Sometimes FREE.* Stand-up shows.

Cosmic Theater Nes 75 (622 8858) *Admission f17.50/E8.* Theatre focusing on different cultures.

Danswerkplaats Amsterdam Arie Biemondstraat 107b (689 1789, www.euronet.nl/dwa) *Admission price varies.* Occasional dance performances.

De Balie Kleine Gartmanplantsoen 10 (553 5100, www.balie.nl) *Admission f10/E4.50 upwards.* Various theatre shows and other events.

De Krakeling Nieuwe Passeerdersgracht 1 (625 3284) Puppet and mime shows, musicals and Dutch-speaking theatre productions for both under- and over-12s.

De Stadsschouwburg Leidseplein 26 (624 2311) *Admission prices vary.* A wide range of productions including theatre, opera and dance.

Felix Meritis Keizersgracht 324 (623 1311) *Admission from f10/*

E4.50. Housed in an impressive 18th-century building, this cultural centre has dance performances and talks as well as theatre productions.

International Theaterschool Jodenbreestraat 3 (527 7700, www.ahk.nl/the) *Admission prices vary*. Regular dance events.

Koninklijk Theater Carre Amstel 115–125 (622 5225) Although the productions staged here tend to be pricey, at 1500 on Wednesdays and Saturdays there are backstage tours of the theatre, costing f7.50/E3.35 adults, f5/E2.25 children.

Muiderpoorttheater 2e Van Swindenstraat 26 (668 1313) Occasional dance events.

Puppet Theatre (627 9188) From May to October on Wednesday afternoons a theatre is held on Dam Square unless it is raining. Then, and from November to April on Sunday afternoons, the theatre is held under cover in St Pietespoortsteeg. There are also shows put on at Amsterdam Marionettentheater, Nieuwe Jonkerstraat 8 (620 8027).

Theater de Cameleon 3e Kostverlorenkade 35 (489 4656) *Admission f5/E2.20 to f17.50/E8*. English and Dutch theatre productions.

Vondelpark Theatre Vondelpark (673 1499) Big open-air theatre with FREE theatre shows and other performing arts from June to August.

Zaal 100 De Wittenstraat 100 (688 0127) *Admission prices vary*. Occasional theatre as well as other cultural events.

Tram Tour

If you are a visitor to the city, a trip on the Circle Tram number 20 is a very good idea. This tram, which begins and ends its journey at Centraal Station, rattles around the city passing many of the museums, churches, bridges and canals. Grab a window seat for this inexpensive tour, where you can hop on and off whenever you feel like it.

The tram runs every ten minutes or so daily from 0900 to 1900 in both directions. There are 31 numbered signs along the route, posted on the signs at the tram stops, on the tram and on the route map.

Tickets are available from the Tourist Information Board, GVB branches, some hotels and on the tram itself. A one-day pass costs f12/E5.40

Views of Amsterdam

Beurs van Berlage Museum (Stock Exchange Museum) Damrak 277; entrance at Beursplein 1 (530 4141) *Open (museum) Tues–Sun 1000–1600. Adults f7/E3.15, children f4/E1.80.* Amsterdam's stock exchange, built 1897, has an adjoining open-air tower that can be climbed.

Kalvertoren (Kalver Tower) Shopping Centre If you'd like to take tea while taking in the view, between Kalverstraat and Singel near Muntplein is the Kalvertoren (Kalver Tower) Shopping Centre. The café at the top boasts a 360-degree view of Amsterdam. The department store Metz and Co's café at Keizersgracht 455 also has a great panoramic view of the centre of the city.

Montelbaanstoren Where the Oude Schans canal meets the end of the Oude Waal is the Montelbaanstoren, a 16th-century gun turret (with octagonal tower added in 1606). The spot provides excellent views over the expanse of water. You get an alternative view of the water by taking a FREE ferry over the IJ, from landing stage 7 or 8 behind Centraal Station.

newMetropolis Science and Technology Center Oosterdok 2 (531 3233, informationline 0900 919 1100, www.newmet.nl) *Open Tues–Sun 1100–1700. Admission ƒ18.75/E8.40.* This popular museum that aims to teach children science and technology in a fun way has a rooftop plaza with great views of the city.

Domtoren, Utrecht If you take a trip to Utrecht, just 30 minutes away by train from Centraal Station, go to the top of the Domtoren, the town's graceful belltower. This allows a good view of the towers and spires of old Amsterdam on a clear day. The oldest you see are the towers of the 14th-century Oude Kerk (Old Church) in the red light district. You should also be able to see the impressively high Nieuwe Kerk (New Church), Zuiderkerk (South Church), the Munttoren (Mint Tower), once part of the town's defences, and the Dome of the Koninklijk Paleis (Royal Palace) in Dam Square. The yellow onion dome is on the top of Amsterdam's tallest tower, on the Westerkerk (West Church) on Prinsengracht.

Westerkerk (West Church) Prinsengracht 279/Westermarkt (624 7766, tower 552 4169) *Open: church Apr–Aug Mon–Fri*

1100–1500; Jun–Aug Sat 1100–1500; tower Apr–Aug Mon–Sat 1100–1700. Admission: church FREE, tower f3/E1.35. This neoclassical church in the Jordaan district was built in 1631 and sports an 85-metre-high (276ft) tower, the highest in Amsterdam, which delivers a great view of the city, though it's a strenuous climb. The tower sways more than an inch in a strong wind.

Zuiderkerk Zuiderkerkhof 72 (689 2565) *Tower open June–Sept, Wed–Sat at 1400, 1500, 1600. Admission f3/E1.35.* Climb the tower of this early-17th-century Protestant church for a bird's eye view of central Amsterdam.

Walking

The most popular areas for strolling, window-shopping and dropping into bars and cafés are the shopping areas around Dam Square, in the old streets around the Nieuwe Kerk, and around Spuistraat on the other side of the square, an area known as Spui. The tranquil Begijnhof courtyard is just here.

West of the centre the Jordaan district is a lovely place to stroll. Originating in the 17th century as a working class area with almshouses built around hidden or half-hidden courtyards, narrow streets and a variety of interesting houses, it now has lots of lovely bars and cafés, boutiques and little street markets.

VVV: The Amsterdam Tourist Office Stationsplein 10, opposite Centraal Station, corner of Leidseplein/Leidsestraat (0900 400 4040, Mon–Fri 0900–1700, and from outside The Netherlands +31 20 551

2525) *Open daily 0900–1700.* The English-speaking staff here can provide leaflets and maps, brochures and information about walks. There are also branches of the VVV at Centraal Station, inside the station at Platform 2 (*spoor 2*) *Open Mon–Sat 0800–1945; Sun 0900–1700.* Leidseplein 1, on the corner of Leidsestraat *Open Mon–Fri 0900–1700; Sat, Sun 0900–1900.* Van Tuyll van Serooskerkenweg 125, Stadionplein *Open daily 0900–1700.* **Holland Tourist Information** Schipol Airport *Open daily 0700–2200* Also gives out walking information.

Gilde Amsterdam (625 1390) A group of Amsterdam residents aged over 55 conduct informal tours of either the city centre, the Jordaan or their own route, giving their own slant on living there. The tours typically last a couple of hours or so and are for groups of a maximum of eight. They ask for an f5/E2.25 contribution (free for under-12s), which entitles you to 50 per cent off admission to the Amsterdams Historisch Museum, the Museum Willet-Holthuysen and a discount on pancakes at the end. Tours must be booked in advance and city centre ones generally leave Tues–Sun 1100 from the Amsterdams Historisch Museum, Kalverstraat 92.

The Association for Nature and Environmental Education Plantage Middenlaan 2c (622 8115) located by the Hortus Botanicus (Botanical Gardens) in the Plantage Organises guided walks.

Let's Go (600 1809) *Jun–Sept, two evenings a week. 17.50/E8.* Organises a two-hour mystery tour of central Amsterdam, and also a 90-minute Rembrandt tour, which includes anecdotes about Rembrandt and 17th-century Amsterdam.

Walking Tour of Amsterdam

This circular walk begins and ends on the Stationsplein, by Centraal Station, and is of about two and a half to three hours' duration.

From Stationsplein, cross the bridge and walk down the Damrak, (the 'Dam Reach') which used to be a busy port but now has more than its fair share of tatty souvenir shops. About halfway is the Beursplein where on the left can be seen the Beurs van Berlage at Damrak 277 Amsterdam's stock exchange built in 1897, an architectural monument with a museum. It was named after H. P. Berlage of the Dutch modern architecture movement. At the end of Damrak is Dam Square which has been the heart of the city since the first dam was built here in around 1270. The square contains the Nationaal Monument a 22-metre-high white obelisk dedicated to those servicemen who died in World War II, the imposing Koninklijk Paleis (Royal Palace) designed by Jacob van Campen in the 17th century, wax museum Madame Tussauds Scenerama, and the Nieuwe Kerk (New Church), built in 1408.

Now return down Damrak a little way and go down Zoutsteeg on the left. Here there are a number of little shops to browse in. Continue up Gravenstraat, which has some antique shops. On the left you come to he back of the Nieuwe Kerk. Cross Nieuwezijds Voorburgwal and after walking via Molsteeg and Torensteeg the Singel canal is reached. The canal used to be the protective moat surrounding the city's medieval wall and has the widest bridge in Amsterdam, the Torensluis bridge that spans it at Oude Leliestraat.

Originally it had a lookout tower and contains cells where drunks were kept in medieval times.

Continuing along Oude Leliestraat, you reach the **Herengracht canal**, which boasts many elegant houses, and then by way of the Leliegracht, the city's widest canal, you reach **Keizersgracht.** If you walk to the end of Leliegracht and turn left immediately you reach the Prinsengracht canal, and soon come to number 263, **Anne Frankhuis (Anne Frank's House)**, where young Anne and her family hid from the Nazis in World War II. A little further on, you come to the **Westerkerk (West Church)** in the leafy Jordaan district, which sports an 85-metre-high tower and a great view of the city. Turn left here, down Raadhuisstrat and on the Westermarkt is a statue of Anne Frank.

When you reach the Kiezersgracht again, turn right walking along its bank towards Hartenstraat. Notice the magnificent canal-side houses with their neck, bell and stepped gables. From Hartenstraat continue walking down Gasthuismolensteeg and Paleisstraat. Turn right at Nieuwezijds Voorburgwal and soon left into Sint Luciensteeg. At the end of this street you meet Kalverstraat, one of the main shopping streets of Amsterdam, where you turn right. At Kalverstraat 92 is the **Amsterdams Historisch Museum (Amsterdam Historical Museum)** and also the **Schuttersgallerij (Civil Guards Gallery)** which has huge 17th-century group portraits and is FREE to enter.

Continue along Kalverstraat until you get to the Spui, where you turn left. Look out for Spui 14, the little archway on the north of Spui Square, which is an entrance to the **Begijnhof**, an enchanting secluded tranquil courtyard of 17th-century almshouses, containing the **Englesekerk (English Reformed Church)** dating from 1400, a Catholic church and, at number 34, Amsterdam's oldest house. Leave the Begijnhof the way you came in, turn right and walk along Spui until you reach the **Singel canal.** Walk left along Singel until you hit the shopping street Leidsestraat, where you turn right. Walk along until you reach Leidse-plein, a square with cafés, restaurants, discos, street enter-tainers and the **Stadsschouwburg city theatre.**

Cross the square, walk straight on and over the bridge and turn left into Stadthouderskade. Across the street you can see the entrance to **Vondelpark**, a spacious park with lawns, lakes, ponds, cafés and gardens. But if you keep walking and turn right into Hobbemastraat you pass the upmarket shopping streets around P. C. Hoofstraat before ending up at the Museumplein. Here are Amsterdam's top museums: the **Rijksmuseum, Van Gogh Museum** and the **Stedelijk Museum of Modern Art**, all with their fabulous art collections. Notice the similarities between Rijksmuseum and Centraal Station at the start of the walk. If you could do with a rest and FREE refreshments call in at **Coster Diamonds** at the corner of Paulus Potterstraat, where you can get a short guided tour explaining the world of diamonds, and have a complimentary drink in their pleasant café at the end.

Go through the gateway under the Rijksmuseum and continue down Spiegelgracht and Spiegelstraat, which has a fair number of antique shops. At the end of this street you arrive at the Herengracht canal again, where you turn right and walk until reaching the Vijzelstraat. Turn left here to reach Muntplein, which contains the medieval **Munttoren (the Mint Tower)**, remains of the old city wall. To the left of the tower is the **Bloemenmarkt**, the famous floating flower market, with its thousands of colourful blooms. To the right of the tower is Kalverstraat, Amsterdam's answer to London's Oxford Street, again. Go down Reguliersbreestraat, on the other side of Muntplein, where you pass the **Tuschinski Cinema**, a magnificent ex–variety theatre built in 1921. At the end of the street is **Rembrandtplein**, the former butter market that is now full of restaurants, cafés and bars as well as Amsterdam's oldest statue of Rembrandt.

Walk further on, down Amstelstraat and cross the Blauwbrug, over the **River Amstel**, which is where the city's name originated – the dam built in the Amstel. Look right and you'll see the 17th-century **Magerebrug (Skinny Bridge)**, made from wood and requiring repairs every 20 years. On the left is the **Stadhuis Muziektheater**, home to the Nederlands Opera and Nationale Ballet, and dominating Waterlooplein. Turn left down Jodenbreestraat, where at numbers 4–6 is the **Museum Het Rembrandthuis (The Rembrandt House Museum)**, which has been recently restored and contains around 250 etchings by Rembrandt.

Continue on to St Antoniesbreestraat, where on the left is the **Zuiderkerk (South Church)**. The former graveyard of this early-17th century Protestant church is now a peaceful square. When it is open, you can climb the tower for a bird's eye view of central Amsterdam. Walk down Zandstraat to the left of the church and then turn right to go down Kloveniersburgwal. Turn left into Oude Hoogstraat and continue on through Oude Doelenstraat. You are now coming into the **red light district**. Turn right and walk down Oudezijds Voorburgwal and you come to the **Oude Kerk (Old Church)** built in 1306 and much altered since then.

Unusually, nearly all the roofs are the medieval originals, and there are 16th-century stained-glass windows and a notable Renaissance facade. Continue to the end of the street and turn left at Prins Hendrikkade and you are back at Stationplein and Centraal Station.

From behind the station you could take a FREE short ferry ride over the IJ. The ferries leave from landing stage 7 or 8 every few minutes, day or night.

Windmills

In the local countryside it is still possible to see working windmills. In Schermer there are three windmills, one of which is still working, and Kinderdijk has 19. Also dotted around the Netherlands are hundreds of watermills, saw-mills and cornmills. Amsterdam's windmills date from the 17th and 18th centuries. Following is a selection.

D'Admiraal Noordhollandschkanaaldijk, near Jan Thomeepad

De Bloem Haarlemmerwed, near Nieuwpoortkade

De Gooyer Funenkade 7 Just east of the Scheepvartsmuseum, is Amsterdam's most central example of a windmill, dating from 1664. It has beer-tastings Wed–Sun 1500–1945 as a brewery is adjacent, tel: 622 8325.

1100 Roe Herman Bonpad, Sportpark, Ookmeer

1200 Roe Haarlemmerweg, near Willem Molengraaffstraat. Built in 1632, this is Amsterdam's oldest windmill.

De Rieker Amsteldijk, near De Borcht

Trips Out of Town

The Netherlands is a compact country well served by roads and public transport so day or overnight excursions are simple. There's lots to see less than an hour away by train or car, and all of the main cities are no more than two or three hours away. The Amsterdam Tourist Office (0900 400 4040 inside the Netherlands) can advise you of ways to get to these places, and most are accessible from trains from Amsterdam's Centraal Station. National public transport information is available on 0900 9292.

Cycling down by the **Amstel river** is popular. If you take the road south out of town along the west bank before long you reach polders and moors, the flat Dutch landscape and some riverside cafés. The days when Dutch ships sailed the globe and its wealthy merchants built sumptuous canal houses are long gone but fortunately they bestowed a legacy of areas of beauty and tranquility all around the countryside.

Two charming old Flemish towns, Haarlem and Leiden, can be easily reached within an hour of Amsterdam and another two, Delft and Dordrecht, lie near Den Haag (The Hague).

Dordrecht has a pretty yacht harbour and a magnificent line of old wine warehouses running along a canal side to the attractively gabled high street.

Delft The centre of Delft features canals and red-roofed houses, and a splendid Oude Kerk (Old Church) and Nieuwe Kerk (New Church) to search out before enjoying a pancake and buying some of the distinctive blue and white Delftware to take home.

Den Haag (The Hague) is where the royal family resides and the government sits, but Den Haag is also home of palaces, monuments, extensive shopping and markets, attractions and the lively seaside resort Scheveningen.

Despite being the third largest Dutch city and its administrative and governmental importance, Den Haag retains an antique, small-town charm. The centre is small and easy to navigate. Its museums include Museum Bredius, with 17th-century paintings by Dutch masters; Museum Gevangenpoort, a former prison and now a museum about justice; Haags Gemeentemuseum, the municipal museum with a varied collection including the world's largest collection of Mondriaan paintings; the Mauritshuis with an excellent collection of 17th-century Dutch paintings; and Museon, a modern science museum.

Queen Beatrix's 17th-century palace Huis ten Bosch and 18th-century Palace Kneuterdijk are not open to the public. Sixteenth-century Noordeinde Palace is not either, although its garden is a public park. The Peace Palace and Palace Lange Voorhout can be visited as can Duivenvoorde Castle in its attractive rural setting. There is a theme park nearby, Duinrell.

Children especially enjoy Den Haag's Madurodam Miniature City. Built on a scale of 1:25 it contains minature versions of lots of sites around the Netherlands including the cheese market in Alkmaar, the Vredspaleis (Peace Palace), the Palace on the Dam, the Domtoren (Cathedral

Tower) in Utrecht, canal houses in Amsterdam and Delft and much more.

Leiden Nearer Amsterdam, the quiet photogenic university town of Leiden is made up of concentric squares of canals surrounding the old town. Here you can walk along the canal sides admiring pretty gabled houses, and discover Europe's oldest botanical garden, the medieval fish market, the corn bridge and churches, and museums of science history, windmills and clay pipes. The area around Leiden has some of the most interesting windmills the Netherlands has to offer.

Aalsmeer A little further north of Leiden is Aalsmeer, where in a huge building the world's biggest flower auctions are held each weekday, the best time to watch being 0730–0900. It deals with four billion flowers and 400 million plants each year. You can watch the spectacle of the auction from the visitor's gallery.

Lisse The world's largest bulbflower garden, the Keukenhof Gardens, is at Lisse. From the end of March until late May each year, this huge park has six million flowers in bloom. It's a fabulously colourful display of tulips, narcissi and hyacinths. There are several themed gardens, imposing old trees, blossoming shrubs, ponds and works of art too. The two main glasshouses contain over 70,000 tulips in 650 varieties. For children there is an animal pasture and play-ground.

Haarlem Ten miles west of Amsterdam and just 13 minutes by train from Amsterdam's Centraal Station lies Haarlem, a very pleasant riverside town built around its almost tram-, traffic- and tourist-free central square, the large and splendid Grote Markt, with a maze of little gabled streets and some good shops, restaurants and the Teyler Museum, which has a collection of scientific instruments and drawings by Michelangelo and Raphael. The Frans Hals Museum contains works by Hals as well as other 17th-century painters. The Muller organ, said to have once been played by Mozart and Handel, is at the late-Gothic church of St Bavo, and dates from 1520.

Zaanse Schans North-west of Amsterdam, Zaanse Schans is a little hamlet on the River Zaan. It has an old-world charm, with white-and-green painted houses and windmills dating from the 17th century, some of which are still working today. There are several museums including the Baking Museum and the Clock Museum and there are also shops, a clog maker and a cheese maker (try some FREE samples of cheese). While you're there check out the relatively untouristy Zaandijk.

Beaches Much of the Dutch coast consists of sandy beaches. In summer you could take a dip at Zandvoort, a popular weekend spot for many Amsterdammers – in fact it is known as 'Amsterdam's beach'. It has a good 15-km/9-mile-long beach, pavilions, surfing and a boulevard. It is overdeveloped, though, and can get very busy at the height of summer and at weekends. Castricum, north of IJmuiden, and Bergen and Egmond, even further north, are far quieter and, although harder to get to, more agreeable.

The coast near Amsterdam also has a nature reserve, the Kennemer Dunes. Bergen, north of Amsterdam, has perhaps the most attractive bathing resort on the North Sea coast, with extensive, uncrowded beaches.

Alkmaar Near Bergen is the picturesque town of Alkmaar, which has an entertaining traditional cheese market in the Waagplein, the market square, at 1000 on Fridays during the summer.

Waterland Just north of Amsterdam around Broek in Waterland and Monnickendam is a region which is rich in lush farmland, ditches and dykes. From Amsterdam you can cycle to it and explore its old wooden houses and farms set in a time warp.

Volendam A village on the banks of the IJsselmeer that has become a prime tourist attraction. Once a quiet fishing village, some locals still wear traditional dress in an attempt to retain the traditional atmosphere. Visitors to the village can dress up too in the traditional costume and be photographed for posterity. There is a museum charting the history of the village and a 17th-century wooden church, and you can learn how to buy and sell fish at the village fish auction.

IJsselmeer Worth checking out along the IJsselmeer are the old port towns of West Friesland, Hoorn and Enkhuizen, which have picturesque old harbours overlooked by 17th-century gabled houses, and the towns of Medemblik and Marken. Edam has some interesting Gothic buildings, and a large church hall, with the Netherlands' oldest carillon, dating from 1560. Monnickendam has some beautiful fishermen's cottages and 17th-century houses.

Wadden Islands For some country peace and quiet (though you won't find this on the beaches in high summer) you could go further north to the Wadden Islands, Texel, Vlieland, Terschelling, Ameland and Schiermonnikoog.

You could visit the most southerly, Texel, on a day trip from Amsterdam, but it's pushing it and it is better to set aside more time for these.

Gooi Eastwards of Amsterdam lies the Gooi region, known as the garden of Amsterdam. Here the River Vecht flows past old farmhouses and windmills, and it is where in past centuries rich Amsterdam merchants built sumptuous country houses. Muiden Castle has a collection of paintings and furniture and the old fortified town of Naarden is worth a visit.

Utrecht In the centre of the Netherlands, Utrecht is about 30 minutes away from Amsterdam by train. It has a large shopping centre, Hoog Catharijne, as well as pretty canals and alleyways. Its museums include Het Catharijne Convent, with the country's largest medieval art collection; Centraal Museum with 17th-century works through to modern art; Van Speelklok tot Pierement, with musical boxes, barrel organs and clocks; and the train museum – Nederlands Spoorwegmuseum.

Rotterdam Rotterdam has the world's busiest harbour and collections here include the nautical Maritiem Museum Prins Hendrik and Museum Schepen Uit Verre Landen, and the arts and crafts Museum Boijmans van Beuningen. There are also changing art collections at the KunstHAL Rotterdam. The Kijkkubussen (cube houses) designed by Piet Blom can be seen by the oldest harbour in the city.

Maastricht The cosmopolitan historic city of Maastricht is at the crossroads of Europe, and boasts inviting pavement cafés and excellent museums. The Bonnefantenmuseum has ancient and modern art while the Museumkelder Derlonj features Romain remains. The Natuurhistorisch Museum Maastricht looks at local natural history and geology, and there are underground mining galleries, a Romanesque cathedral, basilica, Gothic 14th-century church and other monuments and attractions.

De Hoge Veluve and Hoge Veluwe National Parks The heart of the country boasts the huge De Hoge Veluve National Park, which is bliss for cyclists and walkers. It is in Gelderland, an area often overlooked by British visitors to the Netherlands. The nearby wildlife-rich Hoge Veluwe National Park, one of the largest nature reserves in Western Europe, has over 42km of scenic cycle paths as well as 900 white bicycles you can borrow for free. As well as offering endless forest, moors, grassland and sand drifts, the Hoge Veluwe is home to the world's first underground museum where you walk under the root system of a 135-year-old beech tree. Also in the park is the excellent Kroller-Muller Museum (open Tues–Sun 1100–1700), which houses principally 19th- and 20th-century art, an extensive collection of works by Van Gogh and a peaceful sculpture garden.

Arnhem Arnhem is famous for the failed Allied airborne operation of 1944 that led to the deaths of thousands of British and Polish troops. The area contains numerous war memorials, museums and castles as well as the impressive Burgers' Zoo, which boasts a small safari park as well as huge halls housing a mock rainforest and desert.

Apeldoorn Apeldoorn's market, held in the square in the centre of town is a pleasant distraction. Stock up for the week, with wonderful Dutch cheeses which you can taste before buying, delicious meat and fresh fish stalls, beautiful flowers, and – bizarrely – far more stalls specialising in socks than could possibly be necessary. Also in Apeldoorn is the Paleis Het Loo (open Tues–Sun 1100–1700), a summer home for the Netherlands royal family from 1686 to 1975. Now a national museum, its grand rooms display costumes, portraits and other memorabilia, and there are ornate formal gardens.

Giethoorn and Surrounding Area Giethoorn, northwards past Zwolle, has been rather misleadingly dubbed 'the Venice of the North' but is very pretty all the same. The little maze of interlocking canals and fastidiously neat little thatched houses make you feel like you're in a fairy-tale land. At times the village can attract a high number of tourists. Nearby, the pleasant town of Vollenhove has several appealing restaurants and cafés. Blokzijl, which you could also visit in the summer by boat from Vollenhove, is a particularly attractive little village to while away a lazy afternoon. You can explore its compact harbour, maze of alleyways, excellent restaurants and 17th-century houses.

Friesland Further north is the windswept province of Friesland, where half of the sparse population speak their own language, Frisian. Among the vast number of lakes and canals are some enchanting fishing towns and villages such as Sloten, Heeg, Terhorne and Hindeloopen. The larger town of Sneek may have lost its charm, but if you like watersports, it is a must.

Area Index of Selected Attractions

For a description of the boundaries of Amsterdam's districts, see page 12.

Centre

ATTRACTIONS

CAFÉS, BARS AND RESTAURANTS

Grachtengordel

ATTRACTIONS

CAFÉS, BARS, RESTAURANTS

Jordaan

ATTRACTIONS

CAFÉS, BARS AND RESTAURANTS

Pijp

ATTRACTIONS

CAFÉS, BARS AND RESTAURANTS

Plantage

ATTRACTIONS

CAFÉS, BARS AND RESTAURANTS

Museum Quarter

ATTRACTIONS

CAFÉS, BARS AND RESTAURANTS